John

16638
Dear Mom, Get Me Out of Here!

Ellen Conford
AR B.L.: 4.0
Points: 4.0   MG

Dear Mom,
Get Me Out of Here!

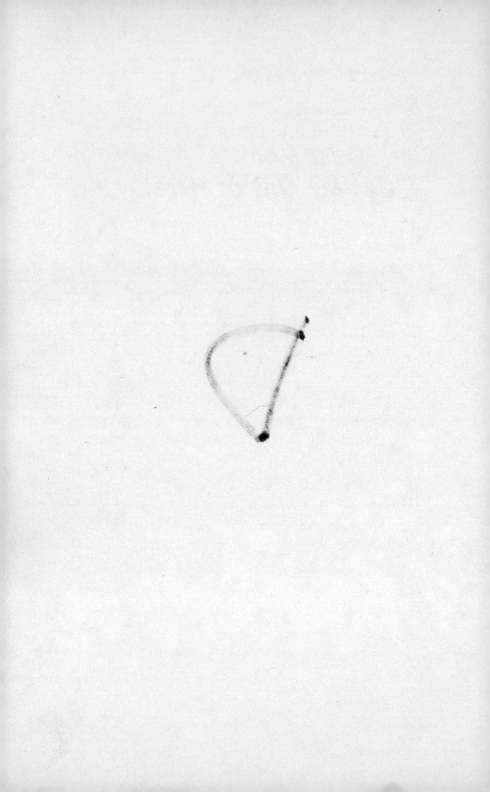

Books by Ellen Conford

Impossible, Possum

Dreams of Victory

Felicia the Critic

Just the Thing for Geraldine

Me and the Terrible Two

The Luck of Pokey Bloom

Dear Lovey Hart, I Am Desperate

The Alfred G. Graebner Memorial High School
    Handbook of Rules and Regulations

And This Is Laura

Eugene the Brave

Hail, Hail Camp Timberwood

Anything for a Friend

We Interrupt This Semester for an Important
    Bulletin

The Revenge of the Incredible Dr. Rancid and His
    Youthful Assistant, Jeffrey

Seven Days to a Brand-New Me

To All My Fans, with Love, from Sylvie

Lenny Kandell, Smart Aleck

You Never Can Tell

Why Me?

Dear Mom, Get Me Out of Here!

Dear Mom, Get Me Out of Here!

Ellen Conford

Little, Brown and Company

Boston   New York   Toronto   London

First Edition

The characters and events in this book are fictitious. Any similarity to
real persons, living or dead, is coincidental and not intended by the
author.

Library of Congress Cataloging-in-Publication Data

Conford, Ellen.
    Dear Mom, get me out of here! / Ellen Conford.—1st ed.
       p.   cm.
    Summary: Trapped in a dreadful boarding school, Paul joins his
classmates in attempting to uncover the shocking past of their
headmaster, Mr. Pickles.
    ISBN 0-316-15370-2
    [1. Boarding schools—Fiction. 2. Schools—Fiction.
3. Humorous stories.] I. Title.
PZ7.C7593Df 1992
[Fic]—dc20   92-438

10 9 8 7 6 5 4

RRD-VA

Published simultaneously in Canada
by Little, Brown & Company (Canada) Limited

Printed in the United States of America

*For my friends in our writers' group—
who have cheered me up, calmed me
down, and spurred me on.*

Dear Mom,
Get Me Out of Here!

1

Paul Tanner stood in the cobblestone courtyard of the Burnside Academy as the black rental car drove away. He watched it until it disappeared through the iron gates, as if he really believed that it would suddenly swing around and his parents would come back and say, "We can't leave you here like this."

But the car didn't turn around, and his parents had left him there like that, standing next to his green camp trunk as if he were just another piece of luggage.

"The boy will be fine," his father had said to Paul's mother. "All he has to do is walk inside. You don't mind, do you, Paul?"

"I'll be okay," he'd said. I don't know anybody, I don't know where anything is, and I've never seen this place before. But hey, don't worry about it. You don't want to miss your plane.

He turned to face the brick-and-stone building. It looked like a medieval castle—or a prison. Four stories of gray stone, long, narrow windows, towers like chess rooks on the corners of the roof.

They probably make you serve detention in the dungeon, he told himself. Chained to the wall. Fighting off the rats for your bread and water.

He couldn't help smiling.

But where was everybody? There wasn't a soul in sight. He scanned the windows. Not a face behind any of them. Not one curious person staring down, wondering who he was.

Had they gotten the date wrong? Maybe the new term hadn't started yet. Maybe there was a measles epidemic, and everyone had been sent home. Maybe the school had closed down since last month, when his parents had enrolled him.

Paul started toward the brick walkway that led to the entrance of the building. He could believe that Burnside had shut down. It almost looked as if it could fall down.

If anybody had replaced the cracked windowpanes or patched up the gouged and crumbling stone walls, they hadn't done so since 1652.

What should have been a broad, grassy expanse in front of the courtyard was tufts of dead brown weeds poking up here and there through a broad expanse of mud.

The bushes were unpruned and half dead, and even the evergreens were tinged with a sickly yellow.

"It's a fine school," Uncle Jack had assured them. "I went there, and I turned out all right, didn't I?" In fact, Uncle Jack had turned out very well. He was a millionaire several times over, and so cheerful and good-natured that it was a treat just to be in the same room with him.

But it was thirty years since Uncle Jack had been at Burnside.

A clattering sound behind Paul cut into the eerie stillness. He whirled around. A blonde girl on a horse was trotting toward him across the cobblestones.

He stared. She had long, fine, straight hair. She was very thin. Even wearing a puffy down vest she looked fragile. Her face was as pale and delicate as a piece of tracing paper.

For a moment he couldn't say anything. Then he raised his hand to wave. "Hi! I'm—"

Her light blue eyes seemed to look right through him. She flicked a rein, kicked the horse's flank, and broke into a canter. She rode past him, across the courtyard to an open field behind the school building.

He stood, frozen, hardly able to breathe. She was the most beautiful girl he had ever seen.

Even as he thought it, he realized that she wasn't really beautiful. And he hadn't been watching girls for very long. He'd turned thirteen in September.

But there was something about her—a white-gold aura that was almost mystical. Paul gazed longingly toward the field. Maybe she'd turn around and gallop back.

Sure. Like his parents' car had come back.

Maybe I'm invisible, he thought. She didn't ignore me. She just didn't see me. No one sees me. That's why there's nobody out here to—

"GERONIMO-O-O!"

The cry came from above him. Way above him. He looked up at the roof. An electric blue figure wearing large, yellow bat-shaped wings flung himself from a corner tower and came hurtling toward him.

Paul gasped. The figure flapped its wings wildly.

"YIKES! HEADS UP! GANGWAY! YOWWWW!"

The flier was rigged up in a contraption of wires and harnesses. For a moment, he actually managed to soar through the air like a human kite.

"LOOK OUT BELOW, DUMMY!"

Paul was so stunned that the only thought in his mind was, I guess I'm not invisible after all.

"Whooaaa!" The boy crashed to the ground, rolling over with the momentum of the fall. Something crunched. Maybe bones, maybe just the wood frame of his wings.

"Geez, didn't you see me?" The boy pushed a pair of aviator goggles up over a snug-fitting cap helmet. "Two feet the other way and my brains would've been splattered all over your face."

"Are you okay?" Paul asked him.

"Okay? I'm a genius. Once I perfect the steering and work out a few kinks in the struts—"

"Do you do this often?" Paul asked.

"Only during lunch hour." The boy got up and held out a blue-gloved hand. A bent wing scraped Paul's cheek. "Orson Autrey," he introduced himself. "Pardon my wing."

Paul shook his hand. The glove was damp with mud. "I'm Paul Tanner."

He couldn't think of anything else to say. What do you say to someone who's just jumped off a roof wearing a nylon body suit, aviator goggles, and bat wings?

Did you have a good flight? Are you acquainted with any other superheroes? or, Exactly how many controlled substances do you abuse?

"Don't you—uh—break a lot of bones?" he asked finally.

"Nah. Mostly I break a lot of wings." He pulled off his helmet and ran a hand through his curly black hair.

"Mr. Autrey!" A voice boomed from an open window on the first floor.

Orson sighed. "Here we go again."

"Who's that?"

"The sworn enemy of scientific progress," Orson replied. "A bitter, frustrated man."

"Mr. Autrey, I want you in my office *at once!*" The window slammed shut.

"Well, let's go," said Orson. "You'll have to meet him sometime."

They headed up the brick walk.

"But who is he?" Paul asked again.

"Mr. Pickles."

7

"Oh." Paul recognized the name. "The principal."

"The head," Orson corrected him. "Headmaster." He pulled open the heavy oak door. "Your first time in private school?"

"Yeah." They stepped into a large reception area with dingy brown tile flooring. The walls were paneled in dark wood. A full suit of armor guarded the empty hallway.

"My seventh," Orson said.

"You've been to seven schools?" Paul asked. "Your family must move a lot."

"No," Orson said. "I just get expelled a lot."

A tall, thin man stood in a doorway halfway down the hall. He wore a black suit and a black string tie. His face was long and narrow. His arms were folded across his chest. He looked like an undertaker. An angry undertaker.

"Did you know," Orson whispered, "that on a boat, head means toilet?"

Paul started to laugh, but swallowed it quickly when he saw the expression on Mr. Pickles's face. With Orson at his side, he probably was not going to get a very warm welcome to Burnside.

Mr. Pickles stalked into his office. He sat down behind a desk and slapped his palms down on the leather top.

"How many times have I told you to stop jumping off the roof?" he demanded.

"Counting this one?" Orson asked. "Four, I think. And I'm not jumping, I'm flying."

Mr. Pickles pointed a bony finger at him. "Furthermore," he went on, "you are not dressed in regulation Burnside uniform."

Paul's jaw dropped. Why didn't Pickles have Orson checked for internal injuries instead of worrying about his clothes?

"I can't fly in a tie and jacket," Orson said.

"You can't fly at all!" Mr. Pickles roared.

Paul jumped. He wondered once again if he were invisible. The head certainly didn't seem to realize he was here. Maybe if he edged toward the door he could make a run for the main gate, hitch a ride, and be back home in Chicago before anyone noticed he was gone.

"I *can* fly," Orson said. "It's just a matter of adjusting the—"

"*Mr. Autrey!* You are grounded. And I mean grounded. You are not to leave your room, except for classes and meals. *And take off those stupid wings!*"

"Easier said than done," Orson muttered. He fumbled with a buckle.

At last the headmaster noticed there was someone else in the room. He shifted his attention to Paul. He bared his teeth. Paul guessed that he was struggling to smile. He was losing the struggle.

"You must be Paul Tanner. It's too bad that your first experience at Burnside had to be an unpleasant one."

"Every experience here is unpleasant," Orson said.

9

Mr. Pickles must have heard the comment, but he ignored it. He sighed deeply. "Under the circumstances, it is also unfortunate that the only quarters for you are with Mr. Autrey."

"Roomie!" Orson threw his arms around Paul's shoulders, smacking the back of his head with a wing.

"Ouch!"

"Sorry," Orson apologized.

How can they be so short of space? Paul wondered. The only life forms he'd seen at Burnside were three people, one horse, and a suit of armor. The building was crumbling, the trees were dying, and the halls were empty.

But he might have gotten stuck with a worse roommate. Orson seemed friendly and good-humored. And he was certainly interesting. He was also probably crazy. But he didn't seem dangerous—unless you happened to be standing underneath him when he tried to fly. And if he kept trying to fly, he might get kicked out of this school, too, and then Paul wouldn't have to share a room at all.

Mr. Pickles came out from behind his desk. "I expected to meet your parents," he said. "Didn't they bring you?"

"Yes, but they had to catch a plane," Paul said. "We missed a connecting flight, and then we had trouble renting a car, and we didn't realize how long the ride from the airport would be."

So they dumped me in the driveway, Paul added

silently. As if there wouldn't ever be another plane to Switzerland if they missed this one.

"Well, welcome to Burnside." Mr. Pickles clasped Paul's hand. "I hope you'll be as successful here as your uncle was."

"Was my uncle a good student?" Paul asked.

"Actually my tenure here at Burnside only began eight years ago," Mr. Pickles answered. "But I'm told he's a very successful man."

"He makes a lot of money," Paul said.

Mr. Pickles spread his hands. "There you are."

"We never met a dollar we didn't like," Orson remarked.

"Mr. Autrey?" The headmaster raised one straggly eyebrow. "Did you say something?"

"No, sir," Orson answered. "Nothing of particular interest."

Mr. Pickles turned back to Paul. "You have a lot to live up to," he said. "I hope you will make your uncle —and us—proud of you."

"I'll try," Paul said. Although if Burnside turned out to be as bad as it looked, his uncle would have a lot of explaining to do.

"Mr. Autrey will show you to your room. I trust that you will not be spending as much time in there as he will."

Orson nodded. "I'm a bad influence." He tried to look remorseful. He failed. Paul pressed his lips together to keep from laughing.

"Your trunk is outside?" Mr. Pickles asked. Paul nodded. "Bucky will bring it up for you. Lunch is just about over, but Swenson will give you something in the kitchen."

"If you're lucky there won't be anything left," Orson said.

The headmaster glared at him. "Mr. Autrey, see if you can get young Tanner to your room without giving him any further negative impressions of our school."

"I'll try, sir," Orson replied. "But it won't be easy."

"Dismissed!" snapped Mr. Pickles.

Orson stretched a limp wing toward the office door. "After you, young Tanner," he said.

At this rate, Orson would be on his way to school number eight before Paul even got his trunk unpacked.

2

Paul lay on his back, unable to sleep. The ceiling glowed in the dark.

"Isn't it great?" Orson said. "It's astronomically accurate, too."

The whole ceiling was dotted with silver stars. And not just stars. Constellations, galaxies, planets, comets with fiery tails, suns going nova, all exploded over his head.

"I did it myself," Orson said.

"Isn't it kind of bright?" Paul asked.

"I used phosphorescent paint," Orson said proudly.

"Why?"

"It's the night sky," Orson said. "How else could you see it at night?"

13

"No, I mean why did you do it at all?"

"You mean, besides the fact that it's extremely beautiful?" Orson sounded insulted. "All the old paint was peeling. What if a big chunk fell off in the middle of the night? I could have choked to death."

"What's that?" Paul asked. "Next to the Big Dipper?"

"It's a naked woman," Orson said. "Geez, how old are you, anyway?"

"Old enough to know that there's no such constellation," Paul shot back.

"Can I help it if the paint happened to be peeling in the shape of a naked lady?" Orson said innocently. "And in case you can't tell, she's anatomically accurate."

"I can tell, I can tell." Paul turned over onto his stomach. He shut his eyes tightly, as if he could force himself to fall asleep.

But he knew he wouldn't sleep. And he knew it wasn't because the room shone with that eerie, unnatural light.

"It took me three weeks," Orson said.

Paul grunted. "Wouldn't it have been easier just to get a roller and paint the whole ceiling?"

"Why should *I* paint the ceiling?" Orson asked. "That's Bucky's job."

Paul gave up. He didn't want to talk anymore. He didn't want to be here. He should have sneaked out of the headmaster's office when he'd had the chance.

And where would he have gone? His parents were on their way to Switzerland. His only living set of grandparents had a one-bedroom apartment in a senior

14

citizen complex. And Uncle Jack was constantly traveling all over the world.

Burnside was home for now.

"Old Sideburns," as Orson called it. "Where the strange meet the deranged."

Paul went over the day in his mind. Classes were over by the time he'd finished the peanut butter sandwich Orson had made for him. It was the last of a small stash of food Orson kept in the bottom drawer of his dresser.

He wouldn't let Paul go down to the kitchen for lunch. "Trust me," he'd said. "Don't start eating the food here any sooner than you have to."

With lunch over, Paul finally heard sounds of life in the halls. From the window he could see boys down on the grounds, heading toward the field where he'd last seen the girl on the horse. A few of the boys carried hockey sticks or tennis rackets.

And one group of six was lugging—like pallbearers at a funeral—something that looked like a coffin.

"Come on," Orson said. "I'll show you around."

"But you're not allowed to leave the room," Paul reminded him.

"How can I show you around if I don't leave the room?" Orson asked reasonably. "And someone has to get you acquainted. A Burnside boy is a friendly boy."

"What's that, the school motto?"

"No. The school motto is Thousands for Pickles, but not one cent for education."

As Orson led the tour, Paul found it easy to believe

15

that Pickles had never spent a cent on Burnside. The classrooms were dim, the books ancient, and every door that Orson opened creaked like something in a haunted house.

The bathrooms were medieval, too. The tile floors had once been black-and-white. Now they were cracked and faded into a dull allover gray. The shower stalls had no doors or curtains, and most of the toilets had no seats.

Paul tried not to sound as dismayed as he felt. "Do you have hot water?" He meant it as a feeble joke.

"Sometimes," Orson said. "Let me tell you, if speed showering ever becomes an Olympic event, we're going to field a great team."

The more Paul saw, the more depressed he got. Burnside was a slum masquerading as a school. He hadn't met any of the teachers yet, but if they had to work here, they must have been booted out of as many schools as Orson had.

"Let's go to the third floor," Orson said. "I'll introduce you to some of the guys. Might as well get it over with."

Paul's stomach churned. What kind of kids would come here? What kind of parents would send their kids here? The ones, like his, who had never seen the school? The ones, like Uncle Jack, who hadn't seen the school in thirty years? The ones who didn't care where their kids were or what was happening to them?

"You have to understand," Orson said, leading the way on the stairs, "that there's something wrong with every kid here. Not one person at Old Sideburns is normal."

"No kidding," Paul said bleakly. "What's wrong with you?" Besides being crazy.

"I told you," Orson said. "I'm a genius."

"You got kicked out of six schools because you're a genius?"

Orson shrugged. "For some reason teachers find it hard to cope with me. Go figure."

Paul didn't want to figure. He didn't want to know anything more about Burnside. He didn't want to meet anyone, not even the pale girl on the horse.

He wanted to go back to his room, pull the frayed bedspread over his head, and hide for three months until his parents got back from Switzerland.

But Orson was already at the top of the stairs. A sign tacked to the first door in the hallway read KNOCK BEFORE ENTERING. THEN GO AWAY.

Orson knocked.

"Go away," came a muffled voice from inside the room.

Orson pushed the door open. "Hey, Bishop, come and meet the newest victim."

"Can't you see I'm working?"

Paul looked around the room. There was no one there.

"How can I see you're working?" Orson asked. "I can't see you at all."

"I'm in my office."

"He means the closet," Orson explained. He pointed

17

to another door. A piece of paper slid out from underneath it.

Orson picked it up. "Chris is editor of the *Burnside Banner*," he said. He glanced at the sheet of paper. "Hey, this is a good one, Bishop." He handed it to Paul.

It was a computer-printed article. At the top of the page, in capital letters, was a headline:

PICKLES FIDDLES WHILE BURNSIDE BURNS.

Then, underneath, in smaller letters:

Deranged headmaster Dudley Pickles did not let the six-alarm blaze that burned Burnside to the ground interrupt his violin practice this afternoon. While students fried to a crisp in the raging inferno, Pickles continued his maniacal quest to perfect "Clair de Lune."

Paul shook his head. "I don't get it. The school hasn't burned down."

Orson snorted. "And Pickles doesn't play the violin, either."

"Then what is this?"

"Looks like the front-page story," Orson said.

"But it's not the truth."

"It's a lot more interesting than the truth," came the voice from the closet.

"But how can Pickles let him—" Paul began.

"Freedom of the press!" shouted the boy in the closet. "First amendment! Nobody censors me!"

Nutty as a fruitcake, Paul told himself gloomily. And they're all like this?

Orson yanked the closet door open. "Bishop, where are your manners? Come on out and say hello to Tanner."

A blond, lank-haired boy was sitting cross-legged on the floor of the closet. A lap-top computer was perched on his thighs. He didn't even look up.

"I don't need any manners," he replied. "I'm a journalist."

Paul felt as if he were groping blindfolded through a maze. "I don't want to bother him when he's working," he said, backing up. "I'll just go back to the room and—"

"And what?" Orson said. "You don't have to do anything till dinner, and after that you'll be too busy throwing up to meet anybody."

"Will you two please keep quiet?" Bishop snapped. "I'm working against a deadline here."

"Let's go," Paul said. He didn't want to hang around Chris Bishop any more than Bishop wanted him to.

"He hasn't really got a deadline," Orson said. "He just puts the paper out whenever he feels like it."

And writes whatever he feels like, Paul thought. What a way to run a newspaper. If Chris was a typical Burnside student, Paul was not eager to meet any more of his schoolmates right now.

He'd go back to his room, unpack, eat dinner, throw up, and go to bed. Maybe in the morning he'd wake up and discover that this had all been just a nightmare.

19

Dinner was just as awful as Orson warned. Watery lamb stew, white bread that tasted like a plastic sponge, and lime Jell-O.

Orson introduced him to the other boys at the table. Their names blurred together. There was a fat boy with watery blue eyes, a boy with flaming orange hair, and a husky skinhead in an army camouflage uniform. He'd been too dazed and they'd been too busy making disgusting noises about the food for him to decide how crazy any of them were.

Except for the fat boy. He wanted to introduce Paul to his pet rooster, Doodle.

Now, in bed, Paul turned over on his back again. How could he ever wake up from this nightmare if he couldn't fall asleep?

He stared at the glowing ceiling.

Even with ninety other boys in the building, even with Orson only three feet away in the next bed, he felt more alone than he'd ever been in his life.

"What do you call her?" He just wanted to hear Orson say something.

"Who? You mean the naked lady?" asked Orson. "Mostly I just call her the naked lady. Hey! You're right. We ought to name her. That's a great idea!"

"Well, it wasn't really my—"

"What should we call her?" Orson cut in. "Let's think . . ."

"Name some constellations," said Paul.

"Orion the Hunter," Orson began. "Leo the Lion,

Sagittarius the Archer, Ursa Minor—the Little Bear. Ursa Major, the Great Bear—"

To his surprise Paul suddenly found himself giggling. "How about," he suggested, "Ursula Major, the Extremely Bare?"

Orson nearly shot straight up in his bed. "That's brilliant! Extremely *bare*. *Ursula* Major. I love it.

"You know, Tanner," he said thoughtfully, "you seem pretty normal, but you may have potential."

"Thank you." But, Paul wondered, potential for what? Did Orson mean that he might eventually fit in at Burnside?

Which would be worse? Turning into the kind of person who belonged here, or never fitting in at all, never making any friends, praying that his parents wouldn't need to stay in Europe any longer than three months?

His eyes blurred as he gazed up at Ursula Major. He squeezed back tears. He wanted so badly to believe that when he woke up in the morning, she wouldn't be there.

And neither would he.

3

BURNSIDE CLAIMS ANOTHER VICTIM!

Thirteen-year-old Paul Tanner, of Chicago, Illinois, is the latest human sacrifice in the unholy war against the innocent youth of America being waged by depraved headmaster Dudley Pickles.

"Hey, Tanner, wake up." Orson shook his shoulder. "Look at this. You're in the paper."

Paul opened his eyes groggily. The nightmare continues, he thought. I'm still here.

Orson shoved a sheaf of papers under his nose. Right beneath the staples was the "Pickles Fiddles" story he had seen yesterday. Under it, in smaller letters, was the article about him.

"Good grief," he said.

"Writes up a storm, doesn't he?" Orson said.

"But how did he find out this stuff? He didn't even notice me yesterday. And I didn't tell anybody where I was from."

"You'd be amazed at what Chris can dig up," Orson said. "This must have been a piece of cake for him.

22

All he had to do was break into the assistant head's office and find your records."

Great guy, thought Paul. He'd probably been expelled from reform school.

He dropped the paper on the bed. "I didn't know he cared," he said sarcastically.

"Aw, Bishop's okay," Orson said. "He's a born liar, and he's a little intense about his newspaper, but nobody's perfect."

Perfect? Paul nearly choked. Nobody here was even semi-sane.

Orson yanked Paul's covers off. "Time to hit the showers."

"It's warm in here." Paul was surprised. Since Burnside provided none of the comforts of home, he hadn't really expected central heating. He got out of bed.

"Yeah, we have heat in our rooms," Orson said. He led Paul down the hall to the bathroom. He pushed the door open. "We just don't have heat in *here*."

The shower stalls were crowded with naked, shrieking boys of all ages and sizes.

"Sounds like a no-hot-water day," Orson commented cheerily.

"Maybe I'll just skip the shower," Paul said.

"You'll have to take one sometime," said Orson, "if you expect to room with me." He handed Paul a skimpy towel from a rack near the door. "Just soap fast and try not to turn too blue."

It wasn't the cold water that bothered him. He'd just never gotten undressed in a group before. The idea of being naked in front of all these people—even though they were naked, too—made him very uncomfortable.

But none of the boys were taunting each other or making fun of anyone else's body parts. They were just screaming, swearing, and rinsing themselves off as fast as possible.

Orson dropped his bathrobe and dashed into the least crowded shower. Paul took a deep breath, pulled off his pajamas, and plunged in after him.

"Yow!" The water was actually almost lukewarm, but in the unheated room his skin sprouted goose pimples the instant the spray hit him.

Orson handed him his bar of soap. Paul shivered and blinked. Orson had already lathered his entire body and was rinsing off.

"Speed showering!" he shouted. He sprinted out of the shower. "You'll learn."

"I don't want to learn!" Paul wailed.

"Then you came to the right school," Orson said.

There were pancakes for breakfast. They were thin as cardboard and no warmer than the water in the shower, but there was plenty of syrup. And after last night's lamb stew they tasted like crepes suzette.

"Hey, Tanner." Chris Bishop leaned across him to get the syrup. "How'd you like my story on you?"

"It was very—uh—creative."

"What do you mean? I got the facts right, didn't I?"

"I do come from Chicago," Paul admitted.

24

"Well?" Chris poured about a quart of syrup over his pancakes. "There you are. Most people are honored to be featured in my paper, you know."

"Oh, I am, I am," Paul said quickly. Life was going to be bad enough without making an enemy out of a pathological liar with the power of the press.

"Don't mention it." Chris waved his hand carelessly. "Just my way of welcoming you to our unhappy home."

Paul learned that the fat boy was named Wendell Warren Williams, and the boy with orange hair, Pinky Lattimore. He didn't ask why he was called Pinky instead of Red. He didn't think he wanted to know.

The boy in the army outfit was Sergio Shapiro. He was still wearing the same jungle-patterned shirt and pants. He didn't speak at all during breakfast. Once he grunted something. Wendell Warren passed him the milk pitcher, and that seemed to be what he wanted.

Maybe Paul would learn to interpret his grunts. Maybe he wouldn't. It was hard to care.

But Paul wondered why he wasn't in the school uniform like all the other boys. Everyone else, except Paul, was dressed in a drab maroon blazer, white shirt, gray pants, and maroon-and-gray tie. Paul hadn't gotten his uniforms yet, but what was this guy's excuse?

Maybe he carried grenades in his pockets and the headmaster was afraid to order him to follow the dress code.

"How do you like pickles for breakfast, Tanner?" Pinky Lattimore asked.

"Excuse me?" Paul looked down at the half-eaten stack of pancakes on his plate as if they might have mysteriously turned into gherkins.

"His little joke," Orson said.

Pinky pointed to a table at the front of the dining room. The head was sitting at one end, along with six other adults, who Paul guessed were teachers.

"Pickles for breakfast, Pickles for lunch," Pinky said. "Pickles with every meal. Get it?"

But Paul hardly heard him. Seated on Pickles's left was the girl he'd seen on the horse yesterday.

He leaned over to Orson. "That girl," he whispered, "next to Pickles—who is she?"

Orson followed his eyes. "Ahh, the mysterious Barbara Catalina. She's Pickles's stepdaughter."

"Stepdaughter?" Paul stared.

"Well, if she were his real daughter, her name wouldn't be Catalina, would it?" Orson reasoned.

Paul's imagination took off.

We have something in common, he thought. She hates her wicked stepfather as much as I hate Burnside. She must miss her real father the way I miss my own parents. Maybe she's secretly longing for someone who understands how unhappy she is. Someone she can talk to. Someone who shares her feelings of—

"Forget it, Tanner." Orson might have been reading his mind. "In the first place, she only has eyes for her horse. In the second place, she's terminally strange."

"Which makes her different from anyone else here?" Paul asked.

"Good point." Orson shrugged and went back to his pancakes.

After breakfast he directed Paul to the assistant head's office. "You'll like Mrs. Stern. I'll never figure out what a nice dame like her is doing in a place like this."

Mrs. Stern's office was opposite Mr. Pickles's. The brass sign on the door read Serena Stern, Assist. Head.

Paul knocked. A musical voice trilled, "*Entrez-vous*, whomever."

Paul pushed the door open. Mrs. Stern was standing behind a desk. A manila folder was spread out in front of her. She looked too young to be assistant head of a school. Even a school like Burnside.

Her gleaming black hair was pulled back into a ponytail. She wore big, round glasses framed in black. She came out from behind her desk, smiling.

"You must be Paul. I was just looking over your records."

She shook his hand, then gave him a quick, friendly pat on the shoulder. She returned to the desk.

"You're pretty bright, aren't you, Paul?" she asked.

The question threw him. "I don't know. I guess I'm just—"

"Well, I know." She tapped the folder. "It says so right here. I hope we can continue to challenge you to be your best."

"It's definitely going to be a challenge," he said faintly.

She surprised him again by laughing. "I meant, challenge you intellectually. Let's work up your class schedule. Then we'll get you your uniforms and you can get started."

With any luck, that might take all morning. He was in no hurry to get started on anything here.

She studied his face. "Don't worry," she said gently. "You're going to be okay."

He wanted to believe her. But he couldn't.

"Really. If you have any problems come to me. Even if you just want to talk. Okay?"

He nodded. Mrs. Stern was very nice, but he didn't think she'd be much help. Unless she was willing to turn her back while he made a break for the front gate.

Getting Paul scheduled and uniformed didn't take as long as he'd hoped. His pants were too long. He had to roll them into triple cuffs, but Mrs. Stern assured him they'd send in an order for his size right away.

By ten A.M. he was sitting in the front row of Miss Bathsheba Twilley's elementary algebra class.

Bathsheba?

Paul tried not to stare. She was shaped like a large figure eight. She wore a red brocade shawl with gold fringe over her shoulders. Her hair was the same color as the dead grass outside, but it had a lot more life to it. It erupted from her head like an explosion in a Brillo factory.

". . . and on behalf of all of us here at dear Burnside," she was saying, "we welcome you. Don't we, boys?" There was general mumbling in the classroom.

"And pity him," added Chris Bishop, who was sitting on his left.

"Thank you." Paul was getting tired of being welcomed. But he appreciated Chris's vote of sympathy.

"We were discussing mathematical expressions of love," Miss Twilley—*Bathsheba?*—explained. "Now, how many of you have heard the song, 'A Bushel and a Peck'?"

Only Orson raised his hand.

"Do you know how it goes?" Miss Twilley asked.

Orson stood up. He began to sing. Loudly. " 'I love you, a bushel and a peck, a bushel and a peck and a hug around the neck . . .' " His voice cracked on the high note. Orson could never claim to be a musical genius.

Paul checked his textbook. It said *Elementary Algebra* on the cover. He checked his schedule. It said "9:45, Elementary Algebra, Miss Bathsheba Twilley." (*Bathsheba?*)

Maybe he would learn algebra at 10:20. ("English, Mr. Roger Pigeon.")

"Very good, Orson," Miss Twilley said enthusiastically. "Now, do you know how much a bushel and a peck amount to?"

"A lot," Orson replied.

Miss Twilley nodded. "That's quite right."

Orson sat down. Paul waited for Miss Twilley to tell them how much a bushel and a peck actually was. But she was already asking another question.

"Does anyone know the poem that begins, 'How do I love thee?' by Elizabeth Barrett Browning?"

Orson raised his hand again. She gestured for him to stand. Once again he stood up, and began to recite loudly. " 'How do I love thee? let me count the ways.' " He really threw himself into it. " 'I love thee to the length and depth and breadth my soul can reach . . .' "

"Very good, Orson!" Miss Twilley sounded as thrilled as if her boyfriend were whispering the words into her ear.

She wrote the words "length, depth, breadth" on the blackboard. Paul groped for a shred of normal classroom structure. He opened his maroon-covered Burnside notebook.

He wrote "length, breadth, depth" on the first page.

When no one could sing "It's Been a Long, Long Time," Miss Twilley sang it herself. " 'Kiss me once, and kiss me twice, and kiss me once again. It's been a long, long time . . .' "

She patted her hair. "How many kisses?" she asked playfully.

"Three," said Chris. Miss Twilley looked disappointed. "You know I'm not good at math, Miss Twilley," he apologized.

"He who cannot count, cannot figure," she said sternly.

Paul put his hand over his eyes. The room seemed to be swimming around. He'd always liked math. He was good with numbers. He liked figuring out things that had definite answers. He liked the challenge of balancing plusses and minuses, of searching for unknown quantities and knowing how to find them.

At school in Chicago, when faced with the problem $x + 3 = ?$ he was always eager to find out what x was.

This was not math. This was not numbers.

This was not a school. This was a loony bin.

Mr. Pigeon (English, 10:20) read "The Raven" out loud. It was a poem by Edgar Allen Poe. Mr. Pigeon didn't sound like an English teacher. He sounded like a mob boss in a gangster movie.

" 'Tis some visitor, I muttered, tapping at my chamber door—Only dis and nuttin' more.' "

Between Mr. Pigeon's Brooklyn accent and the thought of someone named Pigeon reading a poem about a raven, Paul found it impossible to concentrate.

What else would Mr. Pigeon have them read? *Who Killed Cock Robin? Chicken Little? Moby Duck?*

He put his hand over his mouth to keep from giggling out loud.

Mr. Pigeon looked up from his book. Paul looked down at *his* book. But a snicker escaped from between his fingers.

Mr. Pigeon scanned the room. "Somebody wanna say sumpin'?" When no one answered, he continued reading.

Hansel and Grackel, thought Paul. *Huckleberry Finch. Tweety Tweety Bang Bang.* I'm going crazy. I can't help it. Paul dug his fingernails into his palms. Maybe the pain would keep him from cracking up.

31

The bell rang. Thirteen boys leaped to their feet. Several chairs hit the floor. Paul grabbed his before it crashed into the desk behind him.

"Freeze!" growled Mr. Pigeon.

They froze.

"I would like for you to read 'To a Nightingale' for homewoik," he said.

Paul laughed so hard he fell back into his chair. Orson practically had to carry him out of the room.

"Birds," Paul gasped, as Orson dragged him out of the room. "We're only going to read bird poems. *Robin Redbreast Hood.*"

"What's got into you, Tanner?" Chris Bishop asked.

"Pigeon," Paul said. "Raven. Nightingale. Get it?"

He cracked up again. He leaned against the wall, clutching his stomach.

Orson looked at him sadly. "*Tsk.* Only two classes and he's already a pathetic wreck."

"A shadow of his former self," agreed Chris. "Whatever that was."

"*Cheep-Cheeper by the Dozen,*" Paul howled. "*The Yellow-bellied Sapsucker of Texas.*" Tears streamed down his face.

"He's out of control," Orson said.

Chris shrugged. "It was only a matter of time."

Latin I seemed slightly more normal. Since he'd never had Latin before, he couldn't tell if Mr. Waldrup ("Call me Coach") was teaching what they were supposed to be learning.

He was the oldest boy in the class. Mrs. Stern had told him that they began to study Latin in the fourth grade at Burnside. "But don't worry about it," she'd said. "If you need extra help, we'll get you tutoring."

Coach Waldrup did the welcoming bit with Paul, then launched right into the lesson.

"Let's start with today's vocabulary." He picked up a stub of chalk and began to write on the blackboard. Paul opened his notebook.

"Repeat after me: *Periculum*, danger. *Malus*, evil. *Delere*, destroy. *Mori*, die."

Paul repeated each word obediently and copied them down in his notebook. They seemed to be useful words to know at Burnside.

"*Magister*, teacher," Coach Waldrup finished.

Now how did that get in there? Paul wondered.

4

THREE BURNSIDE STUDENTS DROWN IN HIDEOUS TOILET EXPLOSION!!!
GRIEF-STRICKEN PARENTS DEMAND EXPLANATION!!!

"It feels like it's a hundred degrees in here." Paul fanned himself with the latest edition of the *Burnside Banner*. He'd stripped down to his underwear, but he was still sweating.

Orson checked the combination thermometer/ barometer next to his Daffy Duck poster. "Actually, it's only ninety-six. It also says there'll be a typhoon in the next twelve hours, so it may not be all that reliable."

"Nothing works in this place," Paul complained.

"Starting with the teachers," agreed Orson. "Did you try turning off the radiator?"

"The valve's stuck," Paul said. "How come we can't get this kind of heat in the bathroom?"

"Because the furnace doesn't work, either," Orson said. "You open a window and I'll go find Bucky."

"The guy who carried up my trunk?" Paul hadn't seen him since that first day.

"Yeah. He's the janitor. That's why the furnace doesn't work."

"Do you think he'll be able to fix the radiator?" Paul asked.

"I doubt it," said Orson as he left their room.

Paul began composing a letter in his head. *Dear Mom and Dad, I am still freezing in the bathroom but my room is so hot that fungus is growing between my toes and I think I have some kind of tropical fever. I hope you finish your business early and can come home and* get me out of here, *because the conditions are really* . . .

Paul let his mind drift away from the letter. The truth was that after two weeks at Burnside, he was getting used to the place. He was making friends. Weird friends, yes.

But they were warmer and more open than most of the kids he'd met in his first three months of Junior High.

The teachers were weird too, but half of them never checked your homework and the other half forgot what they'd assigned.

And if he didn't stay at Burnside, where would he go? To a school in Switzerland? He couldn't speak Swiss. He couldn't speak any foreign language. Knowing how to say "horse," "spear," and "massacre" in Latin probably wouldn't help him make many new friends. He wouldn't have anyone to talk to except his parents. And they'd never be around, because they'd be dashing all over Europe setting up computer programs.

So there was at least one worse situation than being at Burnside. Though Paul wouldn't have believed it if someone had told him that his first day here.

He went to the window over the desk. At least he could cool the room off till Bucky fixed the radiator. He gripped the sash and tugged.

"Ooof!" He felt the jolt all the way up to his shoulders. The window didn't budge. It must be locked, he thought. He pried at the latch between the top and bottom halves. It turned a little.

He grabbed at the window and pulled again. "Ow!" This time he bent most of his fingers backward and broke two nails. But the window still wouldn't open.

He tried the one over Orson's desk. The latch was frozen shut.

Frustrated, feeling like a boiled lobster, he pounded the window with his fists. It rattled a little, but when he tried to open it again he cracked his elbow against the frame.

He howled with pain. He grabbed Orson's globe and was about to smash it against the window when Wendell Warren lumbered in.

"What are you doing?" Wendell Warren asked curiously.

"I'm severely injuring myself," Paul said. He dropped the globe and rubbed his elbow.

"Why do you want to do that?"

"If we don't get some cold air in this room we're going to sweat to death."

"It is kind of hot in here," Wendell Warren agreed. He plopped down on Orson's bed.

"Did you want something?" asked Paul.

"Orson said he was going to get Bucky. So I came to watch."

"To watch what?"

Before he could answer, Chris Bishop and Pinky Lattimore stuck their heads inside the door. "Is Bucky coming?" Pinky asked.

"Orson's looking for him," said Wendell Warren.

"Oh, good." Chris squatted down near Orson's desk and put his clipboard on his knees. Pinky sprawled out on Paul's bed.

Bucky must be a popular guy, Paul thought.

By the time Orson returned with the janitor, there were nine kids in the room.

Bucky was tall and thin, like Mr. Pickles, but he looked older. He was wearing a brown Australian bush hat and green plaid pants that sagged around his ankles. Over a dingy T-shirt was a peeling black leather motorcycle jacket with a skull and crossbones on the back.

"Yay, Bucky! Awright!" The kids cheered as he lugged his toolbox into the room.

"Got me right in the middle of 'Wheel of Fortune,' " he muttered, ignoring the welcome. "Consarn kids."

Paul wondered why anyone wanted to see such a

grouchy person. He wondered if he had ever heard anyone use the word "consarn" before.

"Danged hot in here," Bucky growled. He dropped his toolbox an inch from Paul's feet. Paul jumped out of the way.

Bucky squinted at him. He had one green eye and one blue eye. His cheeks were covered with gray stubble. For an old guy he looked downright dangerous.

"You new here?" he asked.

"Yessir." Paul nodded. "You carried my trunk up for me."

Bucky tilted his head back as if he were trying to remember. "Oh yeah. Knew you looked familiar. Trunk was danged heavy."

"I'm sorry." Paul wasn't sure what he was apologizing for.

"Can you fix the radiator, Bucky?" asked Orson.

"They don't call me Mr. Fix-It for nothing," Bucky said confidently.

Orson clapped his hand over his mouth. His shoulders shook. Paul looked around the room at the others. They seemed to be choking down laughter, too.

"There ain't a thing broke that I can't fix. That's why they call me Mr. Fix-It."

Pinky Lattimore rolled his eyes. Wendell Warren stuffed the corner of Orson's sheet into his mouth. Paul didn't see anything funny about Bucky except the way he dressed. What was going on?

"Why didn't you open the window, boy?" Bucky demanded. "Haven't got the sense God gave a goat."

"I tried," Paul said timidly. "It's stuck."

Bucky pulled his motorcycle jacket off. "We'll take care of that. Gotta get some air in here." He reached into his toolbox for a screwdriver. He poked the screwdriver around the edges of the window frame.

"There," he said. "She'll open now."

Orson shook his head. *No*, he mouthed.

Bucky gripped the window and pulled.

Nothing happened. Wendell Warren started to giggle but shut right up.

"Goldarn it." Bucky picked up a rubber mallet. He began tapping all around the window frame, hitting the end of the screwdriver with the mallet.

"Bet you got it this time, Bucky," Orson said.

"Yay, Bucky!" Pinky encouraged him.

Bucky tugged at the window. It didn't move.

He turned around slowly and glared at Paul. "You didn't Krazy Glue this or nothin', did you?"

Orson's eyes lit up, as if he wished he'd thought of it.

Paul shook his head vigorously. "No, sir! We didn't do anything to it, sir!"

"You can call me Bucky. Everyone calls me Bucky. 'Cept when they call me Mr. Fix-It."

He reached into his toolbox for a large clawhammer.

"Latch is probably stuck." He gripped the latch with the clawhammer and twisted. "Doggone it!" He grabbed a pair of pliers from his toolchest and fastened them around the latch. He brought the hammer down.

There was a loud crack. The latch snapped and shot up into the air.

"Dang! Almost got it." He raised the hammer again and struck.

Glass exploded from the window. The pliers flew across the room. Wendell Warren ducked just in time to avoid a head wound.

"Yay! Way to go, Bucky!" The kids burst into cheers. Everyone clapped wildly, except Wendell Warren, who was still ducking, and Chris. He was scribbling furiously on his clipboard.

"Dang! Dang, dang, *dang!*"

Paul looked at the huge, jagged hole in the window. Bits of glass littered Orson's desk.

Bucky whirled around and glared at the group. "I hope you're satisfied! Guess it's cool enough for you now."

"Oh, that's much better, Bucky. " Orson nodded. "It's nice to get some air in here."

An icy wind whistled through the hole in the window. Bucky pulled his jacket back on and zipped it up.

"Now I'll fix the dang radiator."

Paul stared at the shattered window, at Orson, at Bucky. Then, as Bucky hunkered down to peer under the radiator, he moved as far away from him as he could get.

"Valve's stuck," Bucky announced.

"Just like the window," Orson said. Bucky reached

for a wrench. Orson moved to the far side of the room, next to Paul.

"This ought to be good." Pinky Lattimore rubbed his hands together. Everyone leaned forward eagerly as Bucky tightened the wrench around the radiator valve.

"I think I got it." Bucky grunted. The radiator made a loud, groaning screech. "Just a little more—"

A geyser erupted from the radiator, shooting sideways and spraying the room with hot water.

"Yippee! Way to go, Bucky!" The cheering boys scrambled onto the beds to get out of the way.

"Goldarn it!" Bucky roared. He rolled away from the radiator. "My jacket's gonna be ruined!"

"Niagara Falls!" One of the younger boys was standing on Paul's bed. He pointed to the water cascading from the radiator. "Niagara Falls!"

"Niagara Falls! " Pinky joined in. Immediately everyone started chanting it.

"Niagara Falls, Niagara Falls!" The little kid started to jump on the bed. Pinky and two other boys joined him.

"Niagara Falls, Niagara Falls!"

"Dang kids!" Bucky screamed.

"Niagara Falls!" All four bouncing boys shrieked with delight as Paul's bed broke and they crashed to the floor.

■   ■   ■

Even with the hole in the window and the electric heater that Mrs. Stern found for them, it took several days for the rug in Paul and Orson's room to dry out.

So when Wendell Warren came to tell them that a toilet had overflowed one morning, Paul couldn't work up much enthusiasm.

"Bucky's on his way to fix it," Wendell Warren told him excitedly. "Don't you want to watch?"

"No thanks. I've seen enough water around here for a while."

Half an hour later, as Paul was re-taping the broken window with a piece of cardboard, he heard loud cheers from down the hall.

Curiosity got the better of him. He headed for the door.

He reached for the knob and as he did, a thin stream of water seeped in under the door.

"Not again!" For a moment he just stood there, staring, as the water trickled into his room. Then he sighed deeply, trudged over to the closet, and pulled on his boots.

5

FANATIC COACH HOLDS PRACTICE IN BLIZZARD!

ENTIRE TEAM HOSPITALIZED WITH PNEUMONIA!!

ANGUISHED PARENTS CRY, "WHAT PRICE VICTORY?"!!!

For at least the hundredth time in three weeks, Paul looked around and asked himself, What am I doing here?

"Here" was the middle of the hockey field. In the middle of a snowstorm. Playing checkers on a redwood picnic table. At ten A.M. On a Saturday morning.

Coach Waldrup believed in fresh air and vigorous exercise. No matter how frigid the air or how pointless the exercise.

He'd led them through five minutes of calisthenics. Then he'd yelled, "Men! Hit your checkerboards!" And for the last half hour, Paul had been trying to play checkers in a blizzard.

43

They were practicing for an upcoming match against Ward Hall. Coach had won second place in the U.S. Open Checkers Championships in 1968. "I would have come in first," he told Paul, "but I was playing hurt."

"What kind of injury can you get in a checkers tournament?" Paul asked Orson.

Orson shrugged. "Hangnail?"

This was ridiculous. Coach Waldrup didn't even seem that interested in the games. While Pinky Lattimore easily beat Paul in their first match, the coach made two calls on his cellular phone and worked a crossword puzzle on his clipboard.

"What's so important that he has to make phone calls from out here?" Paul grumbled.

"He's calling his bookie." Pinky double-jumped and took two of Paul's last four checkers off the board.

"Has he got a gambling problem?" Paul asked curiously.

"Only when his phone doesn't work. King me."

Paul sighed. He was not a very good checkers player. He'd never liked the game very much, and he certainly wasn't going to be an asset to the team. He hadn't even known there was a team until the coach ordered them outside for practice.

But he did find out what was in the coffin he'd seen the boys carrying out the first day. It was filled with checkerboards and sets.

"Why do you keep checkers in a coffin?" Paul asked Pinky, as he, Orson, and Sergio lugged the coffin out to the field.

"Because we don't have a dead body to put in it," Pinky said.

But they would soon. Paul was certain he was going to freeze to death before practice was over.

"Ha!" Pinky cried. "You shouldn't have moved there, Tanner. Now I've got you." He took Paul's last two checkers off the board.

"I didn't have anyplace else to move," Paul said. "And you got me ten minutes ago." He shoved his hands under his armpits and tried to see through the icicles forming on his eyelashes.

Coach glanced up from his puzzle. "Winners play winners and losers play losers," he announced.

As they stood up to switch opponents, Orson blurted out, "This is crazy! We're not going to hold the match outside. Why do we have to practice outside?"

"The cold air is good for you," Coach said. "It stimulates the flow of blood and oxygen to your brain."

"The blood is frozen in my veins," Orson said. "It'll never reach my brain."

"When the going gets tough, the tough get going," Coach said.

"Right," answered Orson. "So I'm going." He started to walk away from the table.

"Autrey! Freeze!"

"I *am* freezing!" Orson howled.

"You get back to this table or you're going to do ten laps around the track!"

"We don't have a track," Wendell Warren pointed out.

45

"I'll draw one in the snow!" Coach threatened.

Orson trudged back to the table. His face was grim. And blue.

"Even the gym is better than this," he said.

"Only barely." Paul shivered. They'd played basketball a couple of times in the gym. The nets were shredded, the baskets bent, the backboards warped. Half the lights didn't work, and the ones that did flickered and buzzed like dying fluorescent mosquitoes.

"You've heard of Madison Square Garden?" Pinky Lattimore had asked him. Paul nodded. "This is Madison Square Weed Patch."

Paul set up the checkers. Either Orson was as lousy a checkers player as Paul, or he was too cold to care what was happening.

Halfway through the game Paul saw, with a surge of excitement, a chance for a triple jump. He reached for his checker and was just about to make his move when Coach's whistle shrilled.

"Time out!" he barked. "Autrey! What's a four-letter word for mangel-wurzel?"

"Beet," said Orson.

Coach counted spaces with his pen. "It fits!" he said, delightedly. "Thanks." He blew his whistle again. "Time in."

Paul rolled his eyes. He tried to remember what his move was. Just as he re-created it in his mind, a gust of icy wind blew half the checkers off the board.

"Not fair!" he yelled. "I was just about to win!"

"Oh, for crying out loud, Tanner," Orson snapped.

"You want to win?" He swept the rest of the checkers off the board. "There. I concede. I forfeit the game. You win. Who *cares?*"

"Not that way," Paul said. "I was *really* going to win."

"You really did win," Orson said. "I gave up."

Paul's next two opponents were third graders. Jonathan Small and David Tomasino. Jonathan was the boy who had helped break his bed. He lost to both of them.

The game with Orson was the only game he won all afternoon.

Paul wrapped himself in his blankets, trying to get warm. But his body felt like a side of beef in a meat freezer.

"I think I've g-got f-f-frostbite." His teeth chattered uncontrollably.

"Well, I think I have a fever," Orson said. He put his hand to his forehead. "I'm probably getting pneumonia."

Dear Mom and Dad,
I am writing to you with the pen in my teeth because my entire body is frostbitten and I can't move anything but my mouth. We had to play checkers outside when the temperature was 24 degrees and it was snowing. I may have to go to the hospital. They are not sure they

can thaw me out here. My roommate probably has pneumonia. But the coach will probably make us play in the match against Ward Hall anyway. . . .

Paul and Orson went down to the dining room with their blankets wrapped around them like mummies.

Mr. Pickles stopped them at the entrance to the dining room. "You boys are not in uniform. We do not wear bed coverings to lunch."

"I'm freezing, sir," Paul said.

"I have pneumonia, sir," Orson said.

"Then perhaps you should skip lunch," Mr. Pickles said, narrowing his eyes. "Perhaps you should both be in bed."

"Oh, thank you, sir!" Paul ran toward the stairs.

"God bless you, sir!" Orson agreed, and wobbled after him.

"Halt!" Pickles raised his arm. Paul expected a bolt of lightning to flash from his bony fingers. "You will get properly dressed, and be back down here in four minutes."

"But we—"

Pickles pushed his cuff back and looked at his watch. "I am counting," he said grimly. "Three minutes and fifty-nine seconds. Three minutes and fifty-eight seconds—"

"Great," said Orson. "When you have to take me to the hospital for pneumonia, they can treat me for food poisoning at the same time."

". . . fifty seconds . . ."

They bolted up the stairs.

They got to their table just in time to see Wendell Warren leap up and run shrieking out of the dining room.

"What's the matter with him?" Orson said, sitting down.

"Chicken nuggets," Chris said.

"He thinks it might be Doodle," Pinky Lattimore said.

"Here comes that man again." Orson cocked his head. Pickles was bearing down on them.

"What's going on here?" he demanded. "What is the commotion all about?"

"It's the chicken nuggets," Pinky said. "Williams panicked. He went to check his rooster."

"Well, confidentially . . . " Mr. Pickles gave an evil little chuckle. "I doubt they're actually *chicken* nuggets."

Paul felt his stomach turn.

As Pickles walked back to the head table, all the boys pushed their plates away. Wendell Warren returned a moment later and sat down, beaming. "Doodle's okay," he announced.

He pulled his plate toward him and started to eat.

Paul tried to fill up on bread and lettuce. His gaze wandered over to the head table. Barbara Catalina was poking her fork around her plate aimlessly. She never brought it to her lips.

Of course, with mystery nuggets for lunch, that was

a good policy. In fact, it was a good approach toward any meal at Burnside.

But she had to eat *something*. Paul tried to send her a thought message. You're so delicate, so pale— if you don't eat—

Suddenly she looked up and gazed straight at him.

Even from that distance he could feel the shock of electricity as their eyes locked. He gulped. A half-chewed crust of bread jammed in his throat.

He tried to swallow, but couldn't. Coughing, choking, his eyes filled with tears. He grabbed for his water glass.

"Heimlich maneuver!" Orson screamed. He lunged for Paul.

Paul tried to wave him away. "I'm all right—just swallowed—" He coughed wildly and swigged down some water.

Sergio Shapiro leaned across Chris and whacked Paul between the shoulderblades. Paul gasped, which just made the coughing worse.

Coach Waldrup sprinted to their table.

"You all right, boy?"

Tears streamed down Paul's cheeks. I'm choking to death, he wanted to say. Do I look all right?

But he couldn't say anything. Just as the coach reached for him, Paul managed to take a deep breath. He exhaled with a whoosh. "Fine," he said. "Okay now." He began to get his breathing under control again.

"Swallowed something the wrong way?" asked Coach.

"You mean, there's a right way to swallow this stuff?" Chris said.

Paul wiped the tears from his eyes as Coach strolled back to his table. Had Barbara been watching the drama of his near-death experience? Had she trembled and turned even paler as he'd fought to save himself from choking?

His eyes followed the coach as he sat down at the head table again. Barbara was gone.

Poor kid, he thought. It was too scary for her. She'd probably run from the room, terrified that he was going to die. She must have been so overcome with emotion that—

"Where'd she go?" he whispered to Orson.

"Where'd who go? Oh, her." Orson smiled knowingly. "To ride her horse. Haven't you noticed? She always leaves lunch early to ride her horse."

Paul put his head in his hands. She'd walked out right in the middle of his horrifying brush with death. She hadn't even hung around long enough to see if he would live.

This was the girl he thought would be his soul mate?

This was the girl he thought he was going to rescue from a lonely, solitary existence?

It looked as if the only way he could reach Barbara Catalina's heart would be to switch to a diet of oats and learn to whinny.

■ ■ ■

Saturday evening the boys were in the common room, watching television. Paul wasn't paying much attention to the screen because Miss Twilley had switched from the news channel to a PBS station that was showing a program on the invention of movable type.

The common room was pretty comfortable, at least by Burnside standards. There was an assortment of unmatched chairs and sofas, some card tables, and a grand piano. There was a collection of board games and jigsaw puzzles, a large stone fireplace, and a stereo set that actually worked.

Nobody else was watching the program on movable type either, except for Miss Twilley. Orson was reading a thick book and making notes in it. Sergio Shapiro was leafing through a copy of *Soldier of Fortune* magazine. Wendell Warren, Pinky Lattimore, and the two little boys who had beaten Paul at checkers were playing poker.

Jonathan and David had huge piles of chips in front of them. Wendell Warren was sweating. Pinky was mumbling curses.

Suddenly Chris dashed into the room, eyes burning with excitement. "You've got to—"

Miss Twilley looked up curiously. "Why, Chris, what's so stimulating?"

"I—uh—solved a really tough math problem," he stammered.

She looked surprised—and no wonder. She never gave any math problems.

"A quick mind is better than fleet feet," she said, and turned back to the TV.

Chris headed for Orson. He bent down and whispered something in his ear. Orson closed his book. Chris yanked at his arm, nearly dragging him out of the chair.

"What's up?" Paul asked as they headed for the stairs.

"Bishop thinks he has a hot scoop," Orson said.

"Shh!" Chris shoved him up the first step.

A hot scoop of what? Paul wondered. Since there was nothing else to do, he followed them up the stairs to Chris's room.

Inside the room, Chris pointed to his closet. It was open. Inside was a tiny five-inch TV on the floor.

"I didn't know we were allowed to have our own TVs," Paul said.

"We're not," Chris replied. "Will you look at what they're showing?"

Orson and Paul squatted down in front of the set.

The picture was black and white, and Paul had to squint to make out the detail.

"It's *Killers on the Loose*," said Orson. "So what?"

"Just watch," Chris insisted.

Killers on the Loose was a show about murderers who had never been captured. Paul had seen it before. Every once in a while there was a story on the news about someone who had been caught because he was recognized on the program.

". . . the house in Minnesota where the grisly murders took place," the announcer was saying, "where Dwight Popper is believed to have slain his wife and two children in a gruesome orgy of blood."

"Dwight Popper," Chris said. *"Dwight Popper."*

"Who's Dwight Popper?" asked Paul, bewildered.

"Look at him!" Chris said. A picture flashed on the screen. Narrow face, close crew cut, long, full beard. Thick, rimless glasses, white shirt, dark jacket, string tie.

"What are we supposed to see?" Orson asked.

Chris smacked his hand to his forehead. "Are you *blind?* Dwight Popper. Dudley Pickles. D. P. What's the matter with you guys?"

"Oh, come on, Bishop!" Orson laughed. "You don't really think—"

"They're the same person!" Chris cried. "The evidence is right in front of your eyes! Mr. Pickles is a murderer!"

6

"Bishop, you've gone over the edge," Orson said. "It's one thing to—"

"It's him," Chris said urgently. "He even has that same stupid string tie."

Paul moved closer to the screen. He didn't really see a resemblance. He tried to picture Popper without the beard.

"Have you seen this man?" the announcer asked.

"I see him every day!" Chris answered.

Popper's image faded and was replaced by the announcer's grave face. "If you think you know this Killer on the Loose, call 1-800-K-I-L-L-E-R. Take no action on your own. Dwight Popper is very probably mentally unstable, and very definitely dangerous. If you can help bring this multiple murderer to justice, call—"

"Get a pencil!" Chris yelled. "Get the phone number!"

"It's 1-800-K-I-L-L-E-R," Paul said.

"Catchy number," Orson remarked.

"I've got to get to a phone." Chris headed for the door.

The picture flashed on the screen again. Paul really didn't think that Dwight Popper looked much like Mr. Pickles, but it was a wonderful thought.

Dear Mom and Dad, And, by the way, Mr. Pickles, the man you entrusted my welfare to, is a homicidal maniac. . . .

"Bishop, don't do it," Orson said. "You're the one who'll get locked up."

"But we're in danger," Chris said desperately. "Don't you see? We're in terrible danger!"

"Not if we don't flunk anything," Orson said.

"This is no joke, Autrey! The man is dangerous. He killed his whole family with an *axe.*"

"So put out a special edition of the *Banner,*" Orson suggested. " 'EXTRA! PICKLES IS POPPER! PUPILS PETRIFIED!' "

"Are you crazy?" Chris demanded. "And let him know I'm onto him? My life wouldn't be worth a plugged nickel. Besides, nobody believes anything I print in the *Banner.*"

"You mean," Paul asked curiously, "you don't expect anybody to believe you?"

Chris brushed away the question like a piece of lint. "We *have* to do something."

"Look, Bishop," Orson began, "Pickles has been here seven years and nobody's been murdered."

"What about Wendell Warren's chinchilla?" Chris challenged him.

"Wendell Warren had a chinchilla?" asked Paul. "*And* a rooster?"

Chris shot him an exasperated look. "Before the rooster. And he disappeared."

"He probably ran off to the woods to look for another chinchilla," Orson said.

Paul was getting more and more confused by the minute.

"If no one believes what's in the *Banner*," he said, "why can't you print the story?"

"Because *Pickles* would know it's the truth."

"You really think it's him?" Paul asked.

Orson groaned. "Tanner, you're not going to get sucked into this, are you?"

Paul wavered. "He could be right," he said. "I mean, if you shaved off the beard—and you have to admit he's kind of strange. He could be mentally unbalanced."

"Everybody here is kind of strange!" Orson retorted. "That doesn't prove a thing."

"I'm going to call," Chris said decisively. "It's my duty as a citizen."

Orson shrugged. "Have it your own way. The loony bin probably won't be any worse than Old Sideburns."

"You watch his house," Chris said. "You can see it from the window over my desk. But don't go out there until the police come."

"Sure," said Orson. "Right. But where are you going to call from? You don't want anyone to hear you."

Chris reached under his mattress and pulled out a Swiss Army knife. "I'll break into his office," he said. "It'll be poetic justice. I'll turn him in from his own phone."

He headed for the door. "What was that number again?"

"1-800-K-I-L-L-E-R!" Paul and Orson chorused.

"Right." He dashed out of the room. They heard him gallop all the way down the stairs.

Orson shook his head. "Pitiful," he declared. "Absolutely pitiful. He's beginning to believe his own stories."

"You don't think he might be right?" Paul asked hopefully. "The string tie? The beady eyes? The same initials?"

"Not a chance," said Orson. "It would be too good to be true."

"Yeah." Paul sighed. And pretty stupid of Popper to use an alias with his own initials.

"But look on the bright side," Orson added. "It's a pleasant way to liven up a dull evening."

Paul and Orson were perched on the desk, staring out the window at Pickles's house, when Chris returned twenty minutes later.

"Did you call?" Paul jumped off the desk. "Are the police coming? No one's here yet."

Chris slumped down on the edge of the bed. His shoulders sagged. He let his hands dangle between his knees.

"They didn't believe me."

"No!" Orson said, with mock surprise. "I can't imagine why not."

"They thought I was just a kid trying to get back at a headmaster I didn't like."

"You *are* a kid trying to get back at a headmaster you don't like," Orson reminded him.

"But that doesn't mean I'm wrong," Chris said. "You'd think they'd want to follow up every possible lead."

"Maybe they got a lot of calls," Paul said.

Chris nodded dejectedly. "Eighty-eight. From thirty-two different states."

Orson sat down on the bed next to him. "Don't take it so hard, Bishop. Even if Pickles isn't a murderer, we can still hate him as much as ever."

"But he is!" Chris jumped up and started pacing around the room. "I don't care if *Killers on the Loose* didn't believe me. I don't care if *you* don't believe me. Pickles is Dwight Popper, and I'm going to prove it."

"How are you going to do that?" asked Paul.

"Investigative journalism," Chris said. "I'm going to dig up everything I can on Pickles's life. I'm going to research the Popper murders. I'm going to find out names and dates and facts."

"That'll be a first," Orson said.

Chris glared at him. "This is serious, Autrey. It could be a matter of life and death."

"I'm all a-tingle." Orson stood up and yawned. "Be sure and let me know how it comes out." He waved carelessly and ambled out of the room.

Chris turned to Paul. His eyes were piercing. "You believe me, don't you, Tanner?"

"Well, I—" Chris looked so intense that Paul didn't know what to say.

"Even if he doesn't go after any of us, what about his wife? And Barbara?" Chris's voice dropped to a hoarse whisper. "Remember what he did to his *first* family."

Paul shuddered.

Barbara Catalina. Not merely stuck with a sour-tempered stepfather, but maybe in danger of being actually *murdered* by him.

All right, Chris could be wrong. He did have an active imagination. But what if this were the one time he was onto something?

All right, Barbara Catalina wasn't interested in any-one without four legs and a mane. But even if she didn't love him (yet), how could Paul just stand by and do nothing when she was (maybe) in the hands of a deranged axe murderer?

"I'm going to need help," Chris said thoughtfully. "This investigation is too big for one person. Even me."

"Well—" Paul hesitated.

"Come on, Tanner. Can't you see the headlines? 'KIDS NAB VICIOUS KILLER—A GRATEFUL SCHOOL CELEBRATES!' "

Paul closed his eyes. He pictured Barbara Catalina, looking at him shyly from beneath her eyelids. "Oh, Paul, you saved me from that horrible man. How can I ever thank you? By the way, I'm selling my horse."

A warm glow spread through his body. If Chris were right about Pickles, it could change the whole course of Paul's life. And if he were wrong? They would only have wasted a little time, and done some interesting research.

It could be a great way to liven up the grim winter term.

Paul opened his eyes. He rubbed his hands together eagerly. "Count me in," he announced. "Now, how do we nail this creep?"

7

Dear Barbara Catalina,
   For a long time I have admired you from afar . . .

No.

Dear Barbara Catalina,
   The first time I saw you I knew that I—

No.

DEAR BARBARA CATALINA,
   YOU MAY ALREADY HAVE WON TEN MILLION DOLLARS!!!!

That ought to get her attention. Paul put down his pen and sighed. What was the point of writing her a letter? She didn't know who he was. And he didn't want to admire her secretly from afar. He wanted to admire her up close. Where she could see him. And admire him back.

At least, he thought that was what he wanted. He wasn't sure, because he'd never felt this way about a girl before. He wasn't even sure exactly what he was feeling. All he knew was that he liked to look at her. And he'd like to look at her a lot more.

Maybe he could send her a letter asking her to meet him someplace. But why would she come? Orson said all she cared about was her horse. Why should she waste time meeting a boy she didn't know when she could be spending precious minutes in the stable?

> *Dear Barbara,*
> *I am writing to tell you that you are in ter-*
> *rible danger. Your stepfather, Dudley Pickles,*
> *is in reality—*

No. Sure, Barbara would sit up and take notice if he said that her stepfather was a mass murderer. But after that, the news that Paul liked her probably wouldn't seem very earthshaking.

Besides, no matter how convinced Chris was, they had no proof at all that Dudley Pickles was really Dwight Popper.

He glanced out the window. A small figure in a blue jacket and cap was walking along the path that led back to the stable.

"Too good to be true," Paul said to himself. What

was she doing out there now? It was four-thirty, and beginning to get dark. There was still too much snow on the ground to ride, even if she could see where she was going.

Who cared why she was out now? He jumped up from his desk. "Don't look a gift horse lover in the mouth," he told himself.

"What?" asked Orson.

"Ha! Good joke!" Paul cackled. He dashed out of the room, leaving Orson staring at his back.

He flew down the stairs, not caring that he hadn't taken his jacket and it was probably ten degrees outside. This was his chance, at last. She'd be alone. (Except for her horse.) Since she certainly wouldn't go riding now, she'd probably just whip him up some oats and hang around the stable for a while.

They'd talk. She'd see instantly how much they had in common.

Paul tried to remember everything he knew about horses.

The yellow ones were palominos. The ones with the big feet pulled beer wagons. Trigger. Hi ho Silver. The Lippizaner Stallions.

Okay, so she'd realize there were other things in life besides horses.

He ran out the main door. She was just turning behind the school building.

They'd arrange to meet secretly every day. (Not necessarily in the stable.) She would open her heart to him. She'd tell him of her hopes, her fears, her secret longings. She'd tell him things she'd never told another human being.

And then, after a week or so, when they were almost as close as two people could be—

Paul picked up speed. He rounded the school building just as Barbara entered the stable.

Panting, the icy air stabbing his lungs, he charged after her. He yanked the stable door open and nearly fell into a heap at her feet.

He caught himself in time and leaned against the wall, clutching at his chest. He tried to control the gross, gasping noises he was making, but it was the only way he could breathe.

She looked at him. There was a tiny glimmer of curiosity in her eyes. At least she wasn't looking right through him, the way she had the first time he'd seen her.

Maybe she thought he was having a heart attack.

Did she care? When he'd nearly choked to death it hadn't sparked her interest.

"What are you doing?" she asked.

"Trying to breathe," he wheezed.

"I mean, what are you doing here?"

"I—uh—" It was getting easier to inhale, but now it seemed hard to think.

"Just thought I'd say—uh—hi again."

She looked at him blankly. "Again?"

"We met before," he reminded her. "My first day here."

"Oh. Are you new?"

Apparently he hadn't made a very vivid impression on Barbara. Of course, he told himself, there were so many other boys here. How could she possibly remember them all? Until she realized how different he was from the others—

But she was already heading for her horse's stall.

He followed her, hugging his arms across his chest.

"Cold, isn't it?" He shivered.

"It's not cold in here," she said. "The stable's heated."

It figured. The bathrooms didn't have heat, but her horse did.

"I meant outside." He didn't know what he meant. He didn't know what to say. He'd better think of something more interesting than the weather, or she'd find him as forgettable as the first time they'd met.

"What's your horse's name?" he asked. And does he always smell like this? he wondered silently.

She unlatched the stall door and went inside. She reached up and stroked the horse's nose. "Noble Warrior," she said huskily. "And he's a beautiful, beautiful boy. Aren't you, Nobie?"

Paul suddenly found he had to swallow. A lot. For one brief, crazy moment he imagined her speaking the words to him. In that soft, cooing voice. Except she wouldn't call him Nobie.

It was really awfully warm in the stable. He concentrated on Nobie's distinctive odor.

"Um, what kind of a horse is he?" Paul asked.

Barbara reached for a brush. "He's a chestnut gelding. Sixteen hands."

Paul had no idea what a gelding was. And as far as he could see, Noble Warrior had no hands at all. But what did it matter if he understood what she was talking about? At least she was talking.

"Do you like horses?" she asked. She began to draw the brush down Noble Warrior's flanks.

"Oh yeah," he said quickly. "I think horses are terrific. Really smart animals."

"Well, they're not *that* smart." She whispered it, as if she didn't want Noble Warrior to be insulted.

"No," he agreed, "not like—as smart as dogs." But they sure are *big*.

"I don't like dogs." She wrinkled her nose.

Paul shook his head firmly. "Me neither."

He'd wanted a dog all his life. He'd never had one because his family had always lived in apartments. But for Barbara he was prepared to forget he loved dogs.

"You're not going riding now, are you?" he asked.

"No, it's too slippery. I'm just going to curry him and muck out the stall."

Paul's family used to eat at an Indian restaurant near his apartment house. It had served curry—curried lamb and chicken. Sometimes, though Paul had never tried it, they even offered curried goat.

Since he was sure Barbara was not going to cook her horse, "curry" must have some other meaning he didn't know about. Maybe they could do it together. Whatever it was.

And he could help her muck out the stall. Whatever *that* was.

"I'll help you if you want," Paul said. "That way you can get done faster."

"I don't want to get done faster," Barbara said. "I like it here."

"Oh." He was stumped.

She cocked her head to one side and looked thoughtful. "But I do have a report to do on Brazil."

"Do you go to Burnside?" Paul asked. "I haven't seen you in any of my classes."

Her laugh was like the tinkle of silver bells. "This is a boys' school, silly," she said. "Why would I go to a boys' school?"

Why would anybody go to this boys' school? Paul asked himself.

"I go to St. Margaret's," she said. "I'm a day student."

Her stepfather might be a deranged murderer, but not so deranged that he'd let her attend Old Sideburns.

"Maybe I could help you with your report," Paul suggested. He didn't know anything more about Brazil than he did about horses. But he was getting desperate.

She sighed and put down the brush. "I guess I'd better get to it," she said. "It's due tomorrow. You really want to help?"

"Sure!" he said eagerly.

"Okay." She eased out of the stall. She pulled down a shovel from a rack near the stable door. "You can muck out the stall for me."

68

"You got it," said Paul. "But—uh—what exactly does that mean, muck out?"

Again, that musical laugh. Her face lit up with her smile.

She pointed to a pile of manure in the stall. "You see that?"

He nodded.

She handed him the shovel. "You use *this* to shovel out *that*."

"What?" Paul stared at the shovel. He stared at the pile of manure. He stared at the extremely large horse standing in the very narrow stall.

He stared at Barbara Catalina. But she was already on her way out of the stable.

"Thanks a lot," she called back over her shoulder. She pulled the stable door closed behind her.

Paul groaned.

What, he asked himself (for the hundred and thirteenth time in four weeks), am I doing here?

Orson couldn't believe Paul was voluntarily going to take his second shower of the day.

"I have to." Paul gritted his teeth. "I can't get the smell of horse out of my nose."

"As long as you get it out of the room, I'll be grateful," Orson said.

Paul peeled off his trousers and dropped them on the floor. They were still three inches too long. He was beginning to realize that he would probably never get a uniform in his size, and that he would spend the next two months at Burnside tripping over his pants.

"Don't leave them there," Orson said, making a face. "Either take them into the shower with you or burn them."

"Relax," Paul said. "I'll put them in with the laundry. If I'm lucky, maybe they'll shrink two sizes."

"If you're lucky, they'll never come back."

Paul's hand was on the doorknob when Chris Bishop shoved the door open, nearly flattening him.

"For Pete's sake, Chris, you—"

Chris slammed the door behind himself and dragged Paul into the center of the room. He looked around furtively, as if spies were lurking behind the furniture.

"There's a book on the Popper case," he whispered. *"Murder and Madness in Minnesota."*

"Super title," Paul said.

"Yeah, well, it's supposed to be in the library."

"There's a library here?" Paul was surprised. No one had mentioned a library.

"In the basement. Behind the boiler room," said Orson.

"But the book isn't there," Chris whispered. "It's listed in the card catalog, but it isn't there."

"Maybe somebody took it out," Paul suggested. "Maybe someone else saw *Killers on the Loose* and—"

"Uh uh." Chris shook his head. "I checked the records. No one ever signed that book out."

Paul couldn't see what the big deal was. "So someone

70

forgot to sign for it. Or didn't bother. Nobody pays too much attention to the rules here."

"You can't forget to sign. And you can't just walk out with a book," Chris said. "One of the teachers is always in the library when it's open."

"Then maybe someone stole it," Paul said. "Sneaked it out under his shirt or something."

Chris began to pace the room. "Why? Most of the kids here don't read anything but comic books. Who would want to steal *Murder and Madness in Minnesota*? Who would *need* to steal that book?"

Paul frowned. He thought he knew what Chris was getting at. "But why would the book be in the library in the first place if Pickles didn't want anyone to see it?"

"Because"—Chris whirled around—"he didn't know it was there."

"It's possible." Orson nodded thoughtfully. "Most of the books are donations from parents. Instead of throwing out their old books, they give them to us."

"And some of the teachers pick up stuff from used bookstores," Chris went on. "Like, two for a buck."

"Must be a pretty bad library," Paul said.

"This surprises you?" Orson asked.

"Picture it," Chris said excitedly. "Pickles is in the place one day, and there, right between *How to Housebreak Your Ferret* and *The Dallas Cowboys Cheerleaders' Diet*, he spots *Murder and Madness*."

"Don't they even alphabetize?" Paul asked.

"Tanner! Who cares? The thing is, Pickles knows

that if someone reads this book, he's dead meat. In the card catalog it says the book has eight pages of photos."

"So Pickles takes it," Paul said.

Chris nodded. "He checks the records and makes sure that no one ever borrowed it." Chris rolled his eyes. "And a good thing, too."

"Why?"

"Come on, Tanner. Put yourself in Pickles's place. You're a Killer on the Loose and somebody recognizes you. What would *you* do?"

"Run away?" Paul guessed.

"No. As long as there was one person alive who knew your secret, you'd never be safe."

"You mean—"

"Right." Chris nodded vigorously. "You'd have to kill him."

Paul felt a shiver go down his back.

"So you can see why I have to get that book," Chris finished.

"I guess so," Paul said doubtfully. "But where are you going to get it?" He wasn't sure he wanted to know the answer.

"From Pickles. And you're going to help me."

"Could he shower first?" Orson pinched his nose.

"Help you what?" Paul asked.

"Break into his house," Chris said.

"Oh, fine," Orson said, to no one in particular. "And they call me crazy for trying to fly."

"Break into his house?" Paul repeated. "*Me?*"

"Us. You wanted to help me nail him, remember?"

"I thought we were just going to do some research!" Paul objected. "I didn't think we—"

"There's nothing to worry about," Chris said. "I have a foolproof plan."

"That's what General Custer said." Orson stretched out on his bed. "I'll miss you, Tanner. Of course, it'll be nice to have a room of my own again."

"Look, what's the worst that can happen?" Chris said.

"You mean, besides getting killed?" Paul retorted.

"We'll be safe as long as there are two of us," Chris said. "He'd never kill someone in front of a witness. Besides, you're not even convinced he's really Popper."

"But you are," Paul said.

"So the absolutely worst thing that could happen," Chris went on, "is that we'd get kicked out of school."

"And charged with burglary," Orson added.

"Petty larceny," Chris said carelessly. "A paperback book."

"Yeah," said Paul. "Yeah! We could get expelled for this!" If he were kicked out of Burnside, his parents would have to let him come to Europe. Where else could he go? They'd have to take him along to France, and England, and Spain, places with heated bathrooms and great restaurants and cushy hotel rooms. . . .

73

He'd miss Orson, but the thought of French food almost made his knees buckle.

Paul sighed happily. He put his arm around Chris's shoulder. "Partner!" he said.

Chris pulled away and wrinkled his nose. "Tanner, what have you been *doing?* You smell *awful.*"

8

LAVISH LIFE-STYLE EXPOSED!!

STUDENTS SUBSIST ON SUBSTANDARD SWILL WHILE PENNY-PINCHING PICKLES GORGES ON GOURMET GOODIES!!!

The checkers match with Ward Hall was a disaster. Paul lost every game he played. The Ward Hall team consisted of fourth and fifth graders, and they beat everybody from Burnside except for Orson and Pinky Lattimore. And even they only won three games between them.

Ward Hall even brought cheerleaders—second and third graders wearing letter sweaters and white flannel pants. Between games they jumped up, formed a circle, and chanted checkers cheers.

"Ward Hall, Ward Hall, rah rah rah!

"King me, king me, hah hah hah!"

They even performed cartwheels.

It was the weirdest sporting event Paul had ever attended.

75

When the match was over, and Ward Hall had won, twenty-two games to three, the cheerleaders led the team in a "Two, four, six, eight, Who do we appreciate? The other team, the other team, 'rayyy!"

Jonathan, David, and Pinky yelled back, "Two, four, six, eight, Who's the team we really hate? Ward Hall, Ward Hall, boooo!"

Coach Waldrup scolded them for bad sportsmanship, but he didn't scold them very hard.

"Well, another humiliating day at Burnside," Orson said as they left the gym.

"Maybe my last," Paul said nervously. "Tonight's the night."

"You're really going through with this?" Orson asked. "You're really letting Chris drag you into his craziness?"

"We just played in a two-hour checkers tournament with *cheerleaders* and a coach who made us massage our fingers for ten minutes before the match," Paul shot back. "I don't think Chris is crazier than anyone else in this place."

And if Chris was right, then Barbara Catalina's stepfather had murdered his children. What might he do to Barbara?

"Okay, okay," Orson said as they reached their room. "I was just trying to keep you from doing something foolish. So when exactly does the caper go down?"

"Dinnertime," said Paul. "Pickles's house'll be empty then."

"You mean, you'll miss dinner?" Orson said.

Paul nodded.

"I guess Chris isn't as crazy as I thought."

Mr. Pickles's house was only a few hundred yards away from the school building, but the two structures were miles apart in appearance.

There was nothing shabby or run-down about the white, two-story colonial where the head and his family lived. Even at dusk, with only a little lingering light left, Paul could see that the paint was fresh, the shrubbery was neat, and none of the windows were cracked.

He and Chris, crouching low, scuttled across the snowy grounds that separated the buildings.

"Are you sure you saw them leave?" Paul asked.

"I saw them go into the dining hall," Chris said. "I told you, this is a foolproof plan."

"Famous last words," Paul said.

"They can't see the house from the dining room," Chris reminded him. "We could walk right in the front door, and they wouldn't see us."

"There's a light over the front door," Paul pointed out.

"I didn't say we *would* walk in the front door," Chris shook his head impatiently. "I just said, we probably could."

In spite of Chris's confidence, Paul's heartbeat speeded up as they sneaked around to the back of the house. "What if there's an alarm system?" he asked urgently. "What if someone gets sick from the moldy meat loaf and comes back? What if—"

"Get a grip, Tanner!" ordered Chris. "There's no

alarm. And they're not eating moldy meat loaf. You don't think Pickles gets the same swill we do?"

"What?" Paul stopped in his tracks. "You mean, we get sauerkraut casserole and—"

"And he gets steak," Chris finished, his eyes narrowing. "And fried chicken. And shrimp. And salad with blue cheese dressing."

Paul was so outraged he forgot he was scared. "That's not fair!"

"Tanner, the guy is a killer," Chris said. "Do you really think he cares about being fair?"

"Shrimp," Paul fumed. "Steak. The man's a fiend." Maybe he wasn't a killer, but he was certainly a rotten human being. He deserved to have his house broken into.

Even if they didn't find the missing book, they might find something almost as incriminating. Maybe he had a stash of dirty magazines hidden under his bed. Maybe he performed horrible experiments on helpless animals in a basement laboratory. Maybe he dealt drugs in his spare time and had a secret bank account in the Cayman Islands.

"I hope we nail this creep," Paul snarled.

"That's the spirit!" Chris approached the back door cautiously. There was a light above it, but it wasn't very bright.

"Considering how many people hate him," Chris said, "you'd think Pickles would have floodlights back here. It sure is easy to sneak up on him."

"Good," said Paul. "He deserves to be snuck up on."

Chris pulled a credit card out of his pocket.

"What's that?" asked Paul.

Chris looked at him sharply. "You've never seen a VISA card before?"

"You have your own VISA card?" Paul was impressed.

"It's not exactly my own," Chris said. "It's my mother's. And it's expired."

"Then what good is it?"

"Tanner, we're not here to shop. This is for slipping locks."

"Oh yeah." Paul nodded. "I saw that in a movie."

"You saw it in a hundred movies." Chris slid the plastic card into the crack next to the doorknob. He bent his head and listened as he moved the card around.

"Got it?" Paul asked anxiously.

Chris pulled the card out of the door. "It doesn't work," he grumbled.

Paul was mystified. "It always works in the movies."

"I can't believe it." Chris shoved the card in his jacket pocket irritably. "I can pick every lock in the school with a hairpin, but this one—"

"Did you bring a hairpin?" Paul asked.

Chris shot him a dirty look. "I'll try the window."

"You can't reach the window," Paul said. "It's too high."

"I'll stand on your shoulders."

Paul looked up. "Hey, it's open!" He pointed. The window was open—only a couple of inches, but open.

"*Now* you tell me?"

"I just noticed," Paul said.

He squatted down so Chris could climb on his shoulders. He straightened up. The ridges of Chris's hiking boots dug right through his jacket into his shoulder bones.

Chris pushed at the window. It slid open easily. "Look at that! Smooth as butter."

"Sure, why not?" Paul seethed. "*He* gets blue cheese dressing. *His* windows open. He probably even has—"

But Chris was already scrambling over the sill into the house. In a flash he had the back door opened. He beckoned for Paul to come inside.

The kitchen was large. There was enough light from a hallway for Paul to see the counters and appliances. Everything was sleek, white, and modern. He had an overwhelming urge to look inside the refrigerator. He wanted to see for himself the brimming shelves of delicacies Mr. Pickles had stocked for his own family.

Chris moved quietly out of the kitchen toward the light. There was no time to case the fridge. Paul followed him on tiptoe. The house was absolutely still. Chris was right. There was nothing to worry about. But Paul tiptoed anyway.

They looked around the living room. "There!" Paul

80

pointed to two walls of bookcases flanking a stone fireplace. "You start on the right side and I'll—"

"Don't be dense, Tanner," Chris interrupted. "You don't think he'd keep the book down here in plain sight, do you?"

"Well, if he doesn't keep it in plain sight, how are we going to find it?" Paul retorted. "We can't search everything."

"The attic," said Chris. "Buried in some trunk or stuck behind the insulation. Maybe under a pile of old newspapers."

"That seems pretty obvious," Paul said.

"You didn't think of it." Chris headed for the stairs. Paul didn't bother tiptoeing anymore. It was plain that there was no one in the house but them.

On the second floor Chris pointed to a trapdoor in the ceiling. A chain hung down from it, but neither of them was tall enough to reach the chain.

"I'll use your shoulders again," Chris said.

"Can't you just find a chair?" Paul asked. "I've still got dents from your boots."

Chris peered inside the master bedroom. "No chairs," he said.

"There's got to be a chair in one of these rooms," Paul insisted. He headed down the hall toward the next door.

He looked inside.

Barbara Catalina, wearing pink pajamas and headphones, was propped up in bed, thumbing through *Horse and Rider* magazine.

They saw each other at exactly the same moment. They screamed at exactly the same moment.

Barbara ripped off her headphones and jumped out of bed. "What are you doing here?"

Paul wanted to throw himself over the banister. Headfirst. But his feet were rooted to the floor. He shrank back against the wall as if he could make himself invisible.

"I, uh—I just—we—"

He looked around frantically. Chris had disappeared. Chris, who had sworn that all the Pickleses were at dinner.

"How did you get in? Why are you sneaking around my bedroom?" Her voice was thin and shrill. Her pajamas had ruffles at the wrists and ankles.

"I wasn't sneaking around your bedroom," Paul protested. *Where was Chris?* He'd gotten him into this. "I'm not even *in* your bedroom."

"Well, if you want to see my father, he's at dinner."

"That's it!" Paul said, with a flash of inspiration. "I saw your father, but you weren't there. So I thought you might be sick."

"I am sick." Barbara pulled the quilt off her bed and wrapped it around herself.

"See, I knew it!" Quick thinking, Tanner, he congratulated himself. "I wanted to tell you I hope you feel better."

"You do?" Her voice grew softer. Paul's heart skittered. He wasn't sure if it was because he wanted to stay and talk to Barbara or because he wanted to get out of there as fast as possible.

"That was nice." Barbara sat down on her bed again.

"So, um—what's the matter with you?"

"A virus, I guess. I have a fever, and I get these chills." She shivered delicately, as if to show him how chilled she was.

"Maybe I could bring you something," Paul suggested. "I could come tomorrow and visit you again. Or if you want me to do anything—"

"You don't have to." She lowered her eyes shyly.

"No, really, I want to," Paul insisted. "If there's anything I can do—"

"That's awfully nice of you."

It might have been only the packed snow dripping from his boots onto the carpet, but Paul suddenly felt like he was melting.

"There *is* something." She hesitated.

"Sure," he said eagerly, "what?"

"Do you think," she began sweetly, "that you could muck out Nobie's stall again tomorrow?"

Paul groaned inwardly. She wasn't interested in him. She didn't like him. She didn't care the least little bit about him. All she wanted was someone to take care of her horse.

"Bucky's supposed to do it, but he's not very—"

They heard a soft thunk from the next room.

"What's that?" She yanked the quilt up to her chin and stared at Paul, her eyes wide.

"That's Chris Bishop," he said bitterly. "He came to see you too. Chris!" Let *him* muck out the stupid stable, thought Paul. He got me into this.

"What's he doing?" Barbara asked.

A moment later Chris appeared in the doorway. "I just came along with Paul," he said. "He was a little timid about visiting you alone."

Paul glared at him. But Chris didn't seem to mind. He wore a secret, satisfied grin, and was patting the front of his jacket. "We'd better go," he said.

"It was really nice of you to come." Barbara eyed Paul. "You won't forget about Nobie, will you?"

If she said "nice" one more time he was going to scream. If she said one more thing about her horse, he was going to scream.

"How could I forget about your horse?" he said dully.

How could anybody forget about her crummy horse?

Chris tugged at his arm. "We *really* have to go," he said. "Hope you feel better."

"You're nice, too." Barbara beamed at Chris.

But Paul didn't scream until they were down the stairs and out of the house.

Then he grabbed the front of Chris's jacket with both hands and stuck his nose an inch from Bishop's. "Why did you try to hide? Why did you tell her I was timid? Why did you say you saw them all go in to dinner?"

"Careful, careful." Chris didn't seem at all disturbed

by Paul's violent wish to kill him. "Don't damage the evidence. It was a natural mistake," he added. "I assumed she went to check her horse, like she always—"

"You *assumed?*" Paul's voice rose dangerously. "You—"

Suddenly he realized what Chris had said. "What evidence?"

"*Murder and Madness in Minnesota.*" Chris reached into his jacket and pulled out a paperback book. He waved it triumphantly in Paul's face.

"You *found* it?"

"While you were cleverly distracting Barbara, I searched the bedroom."

"I thought you were sure it would be in the attic," Paul said.

"But I couldn't get to the attic, remember? So I searched the bedroom instead. And there it was, right in the drawer of the night table."

"Let's see it." Paul reached for the paperback.

"Not here." Chris stuck it back inside his jacket. "Wait till we get inside."

They started jogging toward the main building.

"You know," Paul said, "there could be a perfectly innocent explanation for Pickles having that book."

"Like what?" asked Chris.

"Well . . ." Paul thought for a moment. "Like maybe he didn't take it from the library. Maybe it's his own copy."

"Then who's got the missing library book?" asked Chris. "Don't you think this is a pretty weird coincidence?"

"I don't know," said Paul. "Maybe Mrs. Pickles was reading it. Maybe she saw *Killers on the Loose* and got curious about the case."

"Yeah," said Chris, "and maybe Burnside will get an academic excellence award."

"Well, maybe . . . " Paul stopped short as they reached the front door. He couldn't think of any more maybes. He couldn't think of any other perfectly innocent explanations for Pickles to have stolen *Murder and Madness in Minnesota* from the library.

He gulped. "What if he notices it's missing?"

"He probably will," Chris said. Paul gulped again. "But he won't know who took it."

"Unless . . . " Paul leaned against the oak doors suddenly dizzy with the thought of what they had done.

"Unless what?" asked Chris.

"Unless Barbara happens to tell Pickles that we came to visit her."

9

For two days Paul waited for Mr. Pickles to do something desperate. He slunk around school, expecting at any moment to be arrested, expelled, or, if Chris was right, terminated.

Because Chris's suspicions didn't seem so wild anymore.

Someone had ripped every single photograph of Dwight Popper out of *Murder and Madness in Minnesota*.

Orson was not convinced. "It's probably a second-hand book. Like all the other books in the library. The pictures could have been torn out before he ever got it."

"But it wasn't in the library," Paul reminded him. "Pickles stole it from the library."

"How do you know he stole it?" Orson argued. "Maybe he just walked in and borrowed it."

"He didn't sign it out," Paul said.

"Tanner, he's the head." Orson looked exasperated. "Who's going to ask to see his library card?"

Even Chris was scared—and Paul wouldn't have thought Chris was afraid of anything.

"We'd better not go anywhere alone," he warned. "We have to assume Barbara told him we were there."

"Why don't you just ask her if she told?" Orson said.

"Because that would definitely make her suspicious," answered Chris. "She'd know something was fishy, and she'd be sure to tell."

Orson was growing impatient with them. "Look, it's very simple. Write Pickles an anonymous note. Say that you sent sealed letters to the F.B.I., the district attorney, the state police, and a whole bunch of lawyers. And if anything happens to one of the kids at Burnside, the letters will be opened, and there'll be a big, ugly investigation."

"Orson, you're a genius," said Paul.

"That's what I keep telling you."

Chris smacked his forehead. "Why didn't I think of that? I saw it in a movie once."

"You saw it in a hundred movies," Orson retorted.

"So even if he does notice the book is gone," Chris went on, "he'll be afraid to do anything about it."

"You really think so?" Paul asked nervously.

"It always works in the movies," Chris said. "Well, almost always."

For some reason, Paul did not feel entirely reassured.

Chris printed out the warning note in big capital letters on school stationery and slipped it under Pickle's office door late Saturday night.

"I can't wait to see his face after he reads it," Chris said eagerly.

Paul could wait. For the first time in forty-eight hours he felt that he could breathe normally and stop looking over his shoulder everywhere he went.

He didn't want anything more to do with catching a murderer. He didn't want to know anything more about Dwight Popper. And even if Mr. Pickles wasn't a Killer on the Loose, the less Paul saw of him, the happier he'd be.

They didn't see him at all on Sunday. Paul figured he was scarfing down a twelve-course dinner at some fancy gourmet restaurant in town.

At Burnside they ate cabbage, frankfurter, and rice soup.

Monday morning, David Tomasino came into Miss Twilley's class and handed her a note.

Paul was actually disappointed by the interruption. It was the most interesting math class they'd had so far. Miss Twilley was reading from a book called *Numbers and Your Life*.

She was teaching them how to use their names to figure out their personal numbers. She was just about to tell them how to pick winning lottery combinations. For the first time Paul was learning something useful in her class.

She glanced down at the note. "Paul Tanner. Mr. Pickles wants you to report to his office immediately."

His stomach plunged. Cold prickles spread from the back of his neck down his spine.

Pickles knew. Barbara had told. He'd found that the book was missing, read Chris's note, and put two and two together. (Which was probably more than Miss Twilley could do.)

Any idiot could have figured it out, Paul realized. Why had he let Chris rope him into this? How could he have thought they would get away with it? Would his parents get back from Switzerland in time for his funeral?

"Paul," Miss Twilley repeated, "didn't you hear me?"

He gripped the edge of his desk until his knuckles turned white. He couldn't seem to pull himself to his feet.

Chris's hand shot up into the air. "I'll go with him, Miss Twilley. I don't think he's feeling too well."

"I'm sure that won't be necessary," she said. "David here can escort him to the office."

Yeah, right. David. Three feet tall and forty pounds. Blinking rapidly, mouth hanging open. Great bodyguard.

Paul managed to stand up. As he walked past Chris's desk, Chris tugged at his sleeve. "Don't turn your back on him," he whispered. "Stay close to the door. Play dumb."

I don't have to play dumb, Paul thought. I *am* dumb.

It wasn't a long walk from the classroom, but he felt as if his legs would give way at any moment.

Mr. Pickles's door was open. Paul knocked on it anyway. Very softly. Hoping Pickles wouldn't hear him and would forget that he'd ever sent for him.

The head was standing in front of a window, hands clasped behind his back, staring out at the grounds. At the sound of the knock, he turned.

"Tanner," he said sharply. His eyes narrowed to little pinpoints, making him look even meaner than usual.

"There's a phone call for you. I told your mother you were in class, but she insisted—"

"My mother!" Paul whooped with joy.

Pickles pointed to the phone on his desk. The receiver lay on its side.

"You may take it in here," he said.

Paul ran to the phone. "Mom? Are you back? Are you coming to get me? Are you—"

"Paul! Darling, it's so good to hear your voice."

"You could hear it more often if you wanted," he said, with a little flash of anger. "I've been here five weeks."

"We've been trying, honey. But after we called you the first time, the lines were down because of a snowstorm or something. And once they told me you were asleep and they wouldn't get you out of bed."

Paul forgot he was afraid of Pickles. He glared at him. "They could have woken me up," he said pointedly. "I wouldn't have minded."

"Well, I've got you now," she said, "so let's not waste another minute. Tell me, how do you like Burnside?"

Paul stared at the receiver in disbelief. "Didn't you get my letters?"

"Only one so far. The mail takes five days to get here from the States."

Paul glanced at Mr. Pickles. He was standing in front of a glass-fronted cabinet, pretending to look for a book.

"Then you know how it is," Paul said. Obviously Mr. Pickles was not going to let him talk to his mother in private.

"I know you were exaggerating. It's hard to adjust to a new school. You weren't crazy about the Junior High, either. And everything happened so suddenly—"

"*Mom,*" he said fervently, "I wasn't exag—"

Mr. Pickles strolled over to a file cabinet and pulled open a drawer.

Paul cupped his hand over the receiver. "I wasn't exaggerating," he whispered. "This place is—"

"I can't hear you, honey. But tell me, have you made some friends? How's your roommate?"

Paul sighed. "Fine. Crazy, but fine. He thinks he can fly."

She laughed. "Oh yes, you told me. But I thought you were kidding about that, too. Well, I'm glad you're getting to know people."

He gave up in despair. Maybe when they got his

other letters his parents would realize that his problems at Burnside were more serious than having flaky teachers, a flying roommate, and poisonous food.

But there was no way he could go into details about the danger he was in with Pickles hovering over him listening to every word.

"When are you coming home?"

"We're not sure. I think we can get to see everyone we need to in about six to eight weeks. But even when we do get back it might be a good idea to finish out the term there, so—"

"No!" He shouted it into the phone. "No, it wouldn't! Listen." He lowered his voice to a whisper. "Read my letters when they come, okay?"

"Well, of course we'll—"

"*Read my letters,*" he repeated. "And call me again after you read them. Promise?"

"Of course, Paul. We'll call you again next week."

Next week might be too late.

Who knew what could happen to him by next week?

10

DESPERATE BURNSIDE STUDENTS SEEK SAFE HAVEN AT ALL-GIRLS SCHOOL!!

HORRIFIED PARENTS DEMAND INVESTIGATION OF ST. VALENTINE'S DAY DANCE SCANDAL!!!

"A dance?" Paul's stomach churned, and it had nothing to do with the succotash soup they were having for lunch. "But I don't know how to dance. I've never danced with a girl before. I've never danced with *anybody* before. I don't think I want to."

"You won't want to dance with those St. Margaret's girls, that's for sure," said Orson. "Except maybe"— he leered at Paul— "Barbara Catalina."

Paul swallowed. "She's going to be there?"

"She goes to St. Margaret's," Orson reminded him.

Paul looked over at the head table. Barbara was staring dreamily off into space. Probably thinking about her horse.

Suddenly she caught his eye. A soft, shy smile played

over her lips before she quickly looked down at her food. (Which was probably lobster bisque.)

Paul felt a flutter in his chest—and it still had nothing to do with the succotash soup.

"Whoo!" Pinky Lattimore jabbed him in the ribs. "Did you see her turn on the megawatts? She likes you, Tanner."

Paul ignored him, which wasn't easy because of the sharp pain in his ribs. "And even if I could dance, I'm going to keep tripping over my pants all night . . ."

He still had to roll up his trousers into triple cuffs every morning. No one had managed to find slacks in his size yet.

"Aww, he hasn't got a *thing* to wear." Pinky made "*tsk tsk*" sounds, spurting succotash with each *tsk*.

Sergio looked up from his bread. "I can fix them." He said it so softly Paul wasn't sure he had heard right.

"You can sew my pants?"

"He can sew anything," said Orson. "He makes his own clothes."

Paul stared at Sergio, at the camouflage uniform, at the pockets that might have contained hand grenades.

"He's got a sewing machine and everything," Wendell Warren added.

I'll bet he keeps his scissors real sharp, too, Paul thought. He shook his head in amazement.

"This is perfect, Tanner." Chris rubbed his hands together. "She likes you. You can cozy up to her at the dance and find out if her father suspects anything."

"How can I cozy up to her if I can't dance with her?"

Paul demanded. "Not that I want to cozy up to her anyway," he added hastily.

"Yeah, right," said Pinky. "And I want to stay in Old Sideburns until I'm eighty-two."

"I can teach you to dance," Wendell Warren offered. "I had professional lessons."

Paul suddenly felt as if the room were reeling. Round, lumpy Wendell Warren Williams was a dancer? Next they'd tell him that Pinky Lattimore wrote Miss Manners's etiquette columns.

"We went on a cruise to Bermuda last year," Wendell Warren explained. "And they gave dance lessons every day with a famous instructor. I learned six dances in six days."

"Perfect!" said Chris. "The dance is Saturday. You've got plenty of time."

Paul couldn't think straight. Things were moving too fast. He'd finally managed to convince himself that he should forget Barbara Catalina. He was sure he'd be too embarrassed to dance with anyone, let alone her.

And he certainly wouldn't have the nerve to question her about Pickles. He didn't even want Pickles to see him with her.

"Look," he began, "I really don't—"

She was leaning back in her chair, absently toying with a strand of her blonde, silky hair. She tilted her head to one side. He stared at her perfect nose, her slim, white neck. Her pink lips parted in what seemed to be a little sigh. No matter how devoted she was to her horse, she couldn't bring him to the dance.

"I guess," he said faintly, "I could try."

When Paul saw the crowd gathered in the common room that evening, he nearly turned and ran back upstairs. Half the school had turned out to watch Wendell Warren give him dancing lessons.

Even Miss Twilley, wearing a long, swirly chiffon dress, sat expectantly in the armchair opposite the television set.

"Can't we do this in my room?" Paul muttered.

Wendell Warren shook his head. "Not big enough. Besides, the stereo's down here. We need music, you know."

Paul clenched his teeth. "I am not going to make a fool of myself in front of the whole school."

"Okay, okay. Hey, everybody," Wendell Warren announced, "Paul's a little self-conscious. I'm going to need some more students. Who else wants to learn to dance?"

Jonathan, David, and another third grader jumped up and waved their hands.

"Okay, good. Here we go, Tanner. Now you're not alone."

"No!" Paul hissed. "Not just them." This was humiliating.

"Well, how many more do you want?" demanded Wendell.

Paul pointed to Chris, Pinky, and Orson. "Them," he said. "They got me into this."

Chris shrugged and stood up. Orson bowed deeply. Pinky twirled into the center of the room with his arms over his head, like a toe dancer. "How delightful!" he chirped.

Miss Twilley giggled.

"Now the first dance we're going to learn is the merengue," Wendell Warren said.

"The *what?*" asked Chris.

"Ma-rang-gay." Wendell sounded it out.

"I never heard of it," said Paul.

"Me neither." Pinky scowled. "Why don't you teach us a dance we've heard of?"

"Because this is the easiest one to learn," said Wendell.

"But what's the point of learning it," Paul asked, "if nobody knows what it is?"

Wendell Warren put his hands on his hips and glared at his students. "Who's the teacher here?"

"You are," Jonathan said.

"Right. So let's not have any more insubordination. Once you learn the merengue, the other dances are a piece of cake."

Paul sighed deeply. He had a feeling that the merengue, like everything else he'd learned at Burnside, was going to be absolutely useless.

"All the merengue is, basically," began Wendell Warren, "is eight steps. Eight steps forward, eight steps back." He demonstrated.

"One two three four five six seven eight," he chanted, striding forward. "And eight steps back." He spread out his arms. "Now, what could be easier?"

Paul had to admit it looked pretty easy. It didn't look anything like dancing, and it certainly didn't look anything like any dance he'd ever seen anyone do. But even he could walk eight steps forward and eight steps back.

"Okay, follow me," ordered Wendell. "One two three four!"

"Five six seven eight!" The boys joined in.

Unfortunately, since they were all facing in different directions when they started, they ended up crashing into each other by the time they reached "eight." Jonathan nearly knocked Wendell Warren right off his feet.

Wendell Warren groaned. "It's going to be a long night," he said.

It was a long night.

After the first half hour, Paul wanted to rip Wendell's tape out of the stereo and grind it under his foot. If he heard "Ai yi yi yi, let's merengue!" one more time . . .

And when Wendell Warren made them practice with partners, Pinky Lattimore kept making stupid kissing noises and twittering, "Oh, Paulie."

Miss Twilley volunteered to help partner, and Paul realized that she was a very good dancer. He also realized that Wendell Warren was a very bad dancer. He could do the steps, and he could keep time to the music. But his chunky body was stiff, and he didn't dance so much as stomp. He looked like a fire hydrant with feet.

Paul hoped Sergio sewed better than Wendell Warren danced.

It felt a little strange dancing with his math teacher, but he seemed to pick up the cha-cha pretty easily.

"You're very good," Miss Twilley told him.

"I am?" He was astonished.

She nodded. "You're a natural. All the girls will want to dance with you."

Paul felt his face grow red. Miss Twilley winked at him knowingly. He looked down at his feet. "One two, one two three," he counted loudly. "One two, one two three."

By Saturday Paul had learned the waltz, the rhumba, and the fox trot, in addition to the cha-cha and the merengue. His head was spinning with numbers. The waltz was "*One* two three, *one* two three." The rhumba was "One two *three*, one two *three*."

Once he actually found himself cha-cha-ing to Latin class.

"Nobody dances like this," Pinky Lattimore kept complaining. "Why don't you teach us a modern dance?"

"These *are* modern dances," Wendell retorted. "I just learned them last year."

"But what if they play rock music?" Pinky asked. "Don't you know any dances *real* people do?"

"If they play rock music," Wendell Warren advised, "just hop around and wave your arms a lot."

Sergio measured, marked, and pinned Paul's slacks and returned them Saturday afternoon. They fit him perfectly. For the first time in a month, Paul could see his shoes.

They had an early dinner (potato and sauerkraut casserole) because the bus would take them to St. Margaret's at seven o'clock.

He'd been on edge all day at the thought of dancing with Barbara. When she saw what a good dancer he was, she might forget about her horse for a while. No matter how wonderful Noble Warrior was, he probably couldn't do the cha-cha. But the sauerkraut casserole was an unexpected blow.

"I have sauerkraut breath!" he moaned. He sat on his bed and blew into his cupped hands. "I'm going to breathe sauerkraut on her and make her sick."

"Brush your teeth," Orson said.

"I did! Three times. I still smell like sauerkraut."

With one leg in his pants, Orson hopped over to him. "Breathe," he ordered.

Paul exhaled in his face.

"You don't smell like sauerkraut," said Orson. "You smell like Minty-Fresh Crest. It's all in your mind."

"It's all in my teeth!" Paul wailed. "I can still feel strings of sauerkraut in my teeth."

Chris burst into the room. He was waving a narrow silver bottle shaped like a bullet. He thrust it into

Paul's hand. "Try this, Tanner. It's my killer after-shave lotion."

"You shave?" Paul peered at Chris's face.

"You don't have to shave to use after-shave." Chris said it as if he were talking to a three-year-old.

Paul looked at the label. "IXION! by Paco Dragoon."

"Just use a little," Chris warned. "It's powerful stuff."

Paul opened the bottle. "Whew!" He turned his head away. The smell was weird. A sort of blend of metal, gunpowder, and old leather.

"Just slap a little of that on your face and Barbara'll swoon," Chris promised.

"If I use this, *I'll* swoon," Paul said. But it did have that faint scent of leather, which might remind Barbara of a saddle. And the odor was so strong, it would surely overpower any lingering trace of sauerkraut.

He cautiously rubbed a little on his cheeks.

The Ixion gave him a pleasant tingling sensation, and once it was applied it didn't seem so strong. So Paul dabbed some more on his forehead and shook a few drops in his armpits.

"Whoo!" Chris shouted. "You're going to bowl her over, Tanner."

"But I'm not going to sit next to him on the bus," Orson said.

"Take a good look," Orson advised Paul. Mr. Pigeon, Coach Waldrup, Miss Twilley, and Mrs. Stern led them into the gym at St. Margaret's. "Just so you'll remember what a real school is like."

Paul was too nervous to care about the contrast between St. Margaret's and Burnside, but he couldn't help noticing it.

The gym was a low, modern building of pale brick and huge, gleaming windows. None of the windows were broken.

The highly varnished oak floor was as slick as a skating rink. All the lights worked. There were no dying fluorescent bulbs hissing overhead.

The nets on the basketball hoops weren't frayed or torn, and the backboards looked as white as if they'd never been touched by a ball.

"Look at the decorations," Wendell Warren marveled.

Heart-shaped balloons and cardboard cupids floated above them. Red streamers, pink tissue-paper carnations, and silver hearts hung from the rafters.

"Look at the basketball hoops," Coach said longingly.

"Look at the girls!" Pinky cackled. "Hoo, boy, three babes for every guy!"

It was true. The St. Margaret's fifth through eighth graders formed a crowd of frilly, giggling girls that vastly outnumbered the boys from Burnside.

The two groups faced each other across the gym.

"Remember *Gunfight at the O.K. Corral?*" remarked Orson.

Paul's stomach swooped as he searched the mob for Barbara.

A tall woman in an elegant black dress glided toward the huddle of Burnside boys.

"On behalf of St. Margaret's Country Day School," she said, "we welcome you. We hope that this will be the first of many happy occasions we share."

She shook hands with Mrs. Stern and Mr. Pigeon. Mr. Pigeon looked dazed, and Paul could have sworn he heard him sigh.

"Happy Valentine's Day to all!" She threw up her arms. "Let the dance begin!"

Suddenly music blared from the walls. Loud rock music. Paul looked around for the source. A disc jockey sat behind a bank of amps in the far corner of the gym.

All the boys turned on Warren Wendell. They moved toward him menacingly.

"I don't think that's a merengue," Orson said.

"You can do the lindy to this!" Wendell Warren backed away from his schoolmates.

"You didn't teach us the lindy," Chris said.

"I only had three days!" Wendell cried. "I couldn't cover everything."

"Now, don't panic," said Miss Twilley. "The disc jockey probably has all kinds of music. I'll ask him to play some of the dances you learned."

She headed for the far corner of the gym as the girls began to surge toward the boys like a swarm of bees.

Paul's knees wobbled. This wasn't the O.K. corral. This was a horror movie. The Attack of the Margaret Monsters. *"You can't run from them! You can't hide from them! They will capture you! And they will make you* dance!"

Paul closed his eyes and shuddered.

When he opened them he was surrounded by girls. They were picking off partners one by one, leading them forcefully onto the dance floor. Most of the boys looked as if they were being dragged to the dentist, except for Orson. He just looked bored.

"Do you want to dance?" A girl with short, sleek brown hair was looking up at Paul. Her brown eyes stared into his, as if daring him to refuse. She was already bouncing to the loud, rocking beat.

"Well, I—uh—" He gulped.

Before he could say anything else, she grabbed his wrist and said, "Good."

"Hop around and wave your arms," Wendell Warren had said.

Half the boys were hopping around and waving their arms. They looked like holdup victims who desperately needed to go to the bathroom.

The other half were shuffling their feet and staring at the floor. They looked miserable.

"I don't really know how to dance," Paul said. "At least, not this way."

"Doesn't matter," the girl said. "Just do whatever you feel like doing to the rhythm of the music."

He didn't feel like doing anything to the rhythm of that music, but the girl started jumping and jiggling and twisting. Her eyes were half closed, as if she didn't care whether he were there or not.

Well, he couldn't look any stupider than the rest of his classmates. So he shrugged and began to jump and jiggle alongside her.

But he kept his eyes open and searched the room for Barbara.

He spotted her just as the music stopped. She was with Chris. She was wearing a white dress, white stockings, and black patent-leather shoes with little heels.

Chris pointed at Paul and started to pull her toward him.

"You're not such a bad dancer," the girl with the brown hair said. "You want to dance again?"

Paul hardly heard her.

"Paul's been looking all over for you," Chris said to Barbara as they met in the middle of the gym. Paul felt his face start to flush.

"Oh, he was not," Barbara said. "He was dancing with Cindy."

Suddenly a burst of familiar music erupted from the speakers. "*Ai yi yi yi yi mer-en-gue!*"

There was a roar from the Burnside group, and the boys started to sing along with the music, almost drowning it out.

Most of the St. Margaret's girls looked completely mystified. Barbara tilted her head to one side and frowned.

"What is this?" she asked.

"It's a merengue," said Chris. "Ma-rang-gay."

"I don't know any dance like that." She looked irritated.

"Paul can teach you. He's an expert merengue-er." Chris practically shoved Paul and Barbara into each others' arms. Already some of the other boys were demonstrating Wendell Warren's version of the merengue to their partners, with a great deal of stomping and clumping.

Chris leaned over and hissed into Paul's ear. "Now or never, Tanner."

Paul cleared his throat and tried to sound confident. "It's very easy," he told Barbara. "The whole dance is only eight steps." Boldly, he took her hand.

She held back for a moment, then let him lead her into the first steps of the dance.

Somehow, Paul had imagined that they would glide smoothly across the floor, falling into perfect rhythm with each other, lost in a world of music and romance.

Somehow he had never imagined that slim, beautiful, mystical Barbara Catalina would be a lousy dancer.

But she was. No matter how easy Wendell Warren had claimed the merengue was, she just couldn't get the hang of it. Either she didn't know how to count to eight, or she didn't know the difference between forward and backward.

Or maybe Paul's Ixion contained some sort of nerve gas that interfered with muscle coordination.

She got flustered, frustrated, and sulky. By the time the merengue ended, Paul felt like a bully for putting her through such torture.

"I'm sorry," she snapped, when the music stopped. "I just can't do that dance."

He stood helplessly next to her, watching her chew on her lip. "Maybe they'll play something you—"

The music started again, and again the boys roared with appreciation.

"Cha-cha!"

Barbara's face grew grim. Some of the girls recognized the cha-cha. The gym floor began to resound with the "one two, one two three" beat.

"What's the *matter* with that disc jockey?" Barbara fumed. "I'm going to get him to play some *real* music." She whirled around and stalked off. Before Paul could blink, he was surrounded by four girls. One of them was Cindy.

"You sure are a good dancer," she said.

"Would you teach me—" Two other girls started to ask at the same time.

"Sure, I'll—"

But Cindy grabbed him. "I know how to cha-cha," she said. She turned over her shoulder to the other girls. "You watch us first."

Cindy did know how to cha-cha, but she took the boy's lead part, which threw Paul for a moment.

But he adjusted, switched direction, and let her lead. He looked around for Barbara, but didn't see her.

"That's interesting cologne you've got on," Cindy said. One two three.

"It's not cologne," Paul told her. "It's after-shave."

"You *shave?*" Cindy seemed very impressed.

"Well," he said nonchalantly, "not every day." One two three.

Barbara could wait, he decided. He was practically

the Fred Astaire of Burnside, and all these girls were fighting each other for a chance to dance with him.

He'd catch her later.

But he didn't. If he was the Fred Astaire of Burnside, an awful lot of girls wanted to be his Ginger Rogers. Was it Chris's killer after-shave? Or was he really the best dancer on the floor? Maybe he was better looking than he'd ever thought he was.

Or maybe it was because, as Pinky had observed, there were three girls to every boy.

Whatever the reason, Paul couldn't even drink a glass of punch without five girls offering him cookies, and then waiting for him to finish swallowing so he could dance again.

Finally the beautiful woman in the black dress announced the last dance. Cindy and five other girls sprinted toward Paul. He scanned the gym for Barbara. He realized with a little twinge of guilt that he'd hardly thought about her for the last two hours.

At last he picked her out of the crowd. But she wasn't alone. She wasn't waiting for him. She was standing arm-in-arm with Chris.

"Last dance, Paul," all five girls said together.

He was glad he didn't have to choose. Once again, Cindy had the quickest reflexes and the most direct approach. She simply grabbed his arm and bent it around her waist.

"I'm glad this is a slow dance," she said. "I mean,

I like rock, but I think the last dance should be slow, don't you?"

She even let him lead this time. Paul glanced over at Chris and Barbara. Barbara wasn't even good at slow dancing!

Too much time on her horse, he figured, and not enough practice standing on her own two feet.

Her two left feet.

With an extra-special flourish, he twirled Cindy under his arm.

There wasn't any applause, but in his mind he heard it anyway.

11

PICKLES PINCHES PUPIL'S PET FOR BIZARRE MEDICAL EXPERIMENTS!

CRAZED HEADMASTER SELLS ROOSTER TO ROVING BAND OF MAD SCIENTISTS!!

Dear Paul,

I'm sorry I didn't get to talk to you the other day, but I was en route back to Switzerland from Germany when your mother finally got through to you.

I don't understand why phoning should be such a problem, but it seems as if every time we try to call we have trouble reaching the school, or you're not available. Your mother was very relieved to talk to you in person again.

I know it's hard to adjust to a new situation, especially to one that happened so suddenly. When we got your first couple of letters we thought you might be exaggerating about the conditions at Burnside. We thought you might *feel resentment or anger at us for sending you there. Or that maybe you were just having fun, making jokes about the school to liven up your letters.*

But your mother said you told her to take your letters seriously, and we're beginning to get worried.

No matter what Uncle Jack said, no matter how fast we had to make arrangements, we should have investigated Burnside more thoroughly. We should have visited it ourselves before we left you there. We realize that now.

So, in two weeks we're going to do what we should have done in the first place. We're coming to see you—and Burnside—for ourselves. We'll be there the first week in March. I can't give you the exact date, but don't worry. We'll be there.

We're not telling Mr. Pickles that we're coming. We want to see what the school is like when they're not expecting company.

And we can't wait to see you!

Love,
Dad

Paul read the letter with mixed feelings. Since the dance at St. Margaret's his attitude toward Burnside had turned oddly mellow.

The day after the dance Miss Twilley declared that he'd been "the beau of the ball." He didn't know what she meant until Orson explained that it was the male version of the belle of the ball—the most popular person at the dance.

And all the boys were sharing in Paul's triumph. Chris insisted that it was his after-shave that made Paul irresistible. Wendell Warren said it was the dancing lessons. Sergio didn't say anything, but Paul told everyone that if Sergio hadn't shortened his trousers, he would have been the buffoon of the ball.

Pinky Lattimore even took to calling him "Killer."

Mr. Pigeon started studying love letters in English class. When he read them aloud, his Brooklyn gangster voice softened, and he got a misty, faraway look in his eyes.

He had them make up their own love letters. Pinky's letter was: *"Dear Michelle Pfeiffer, will you marry me?"*

Paul discovered he had no desire to write love letters to Barbara Catalina anymore. He could never, he realized, get serious about a girl who was such a bad dancer. He found himself thinking about Cindy a lot. About her dark, gleaming hair, and the way her strong fingers claimed his wrist.

Which was just as well, because Chris told him that Barbara didn't even remember his name. He'd found out that she'd never told Pickles they'd been in the house. Which was also just as well, because Chris had just finished speed-reading *Murder and Madness in Minnesota* and was more convinced than ever that Pickles was Dwight Popper.

But now that he knew Pickles had no reason to be suspicious of him, Paul stopped looking over his shoulder every time he walked down the hall.

He was too busy passing around a petition to schedule a St. Patrick's Day dance.

He'd be happy to see his parents, but he was getting used to Burnside and actually becoming fond of the strange collection of people he lived with.

He put down his father's letter and looked over at Orson. His roommate was making a new set of wings out of a bolt of material Sergio had ordered from his Wide World of Fabrics catalog.

"Spandex, Tanner." He and Sergio stretched out the tape measure. "The fabric of the future. Light, resilient, retains its shape no matter what."

Paul shook his head. "I'm going to miss you when you're dead, Orson."

"This stuff is going to work," Orson insisted. "It'll stretch with the wind, it'll never tear. And if I get snagged on a tree branch, the worst that can happen is I'll dangle there for a while until someone comes to rescue me."

"Well, that's something to look forward to," Paul said. "Seeing you dangling from a tree."

"Oh, ye of little faith," Orson sighed. "We geniuses are never appreciated in our—"

The door flew open and crashed against the wall behind it. Wendell Warren, eyes wide, face pale with terror, clutched at his chest. He looked as if he was having a heart attack.

"What's the matter?" asked Paul, startled.

"It's Doodle," Wendell Warren gasped. "He's gone."

"Your rooster?" Orson began to trace a pattern on the Spandex with chalk. He didn't sound very concerned.

"Probably went looking for a chicken."

"Doodle loved me!" Wendell cried. "He would never have left of his own free will!"

"You mean, you suspect fowl play?" Orson raised an eyebrow. "Get it, Wendell, *fowl* play?"

"It's not funny!" he wailed.

"Hey, Orson, he's really upset," said Paul. "Don't make jokes."

"Well, *excuse* me," Orson retorted. "But I can only concentrate on one set of wings at a time."

"When did you last see him?" asked Paul.

"Before lunch." Wendell Warren's eyes filled with tears. "When I came back to my room his cage was open and he was gone."

"Has he seemed depressed lately?" Orson asked.

"Cut it out!" Paul glared at his roommate.

"We could get up a reconnaissance mission." Sergio said it so quietly Paul hardly heard him.

"A what?" sniffled Wendell.

"A search party," explained Paul. "We'll get everybody together and go look for Doodle. I'll help." He turned to Sergio. "You're probably very good at this kind of thing."

Sergio shrugged modestly. "I know a little about reconnaissance."

115

"And Orson will help," Paul added.

Orson looked down at his wing pattern. He sighed. "Oh, well, birds of a feather, I guess . . . "

A sudden warm spell had melted most of the snow on the Burnside campus, leaving the ground soft and muddy. The twenty boys gathered in front of the building had some interesting ideas about the proper dress for a search party.

Sergio, of course, wore his camouflage uniform. Somewhere Orson had found a deerstalker cap and a long black cloak. He looked like a cross between Sherlock Holmes and Dracula.

Pinky Lattimore wore a black watch cap, black pants, black boots, black leather gloves, and a green T-shirt that read KISS ME, I'M IRISH.

Most of the younger boys were dressed more normally, except for Jonathan. He wore a pith helmet and sunglasses. And David, the other third grader who had beaten Paul at checkers, was wearing a Baltimore Orioles baseball uniform, complete with chest protector and catcher's mitt.

Paul pointed him out to Orson. "Think he's hoping to catch Doodle on the fly?" he asked. "Or maybe he thinks if he dresses like a bird—"

"Don't make jokes," Orson said sourly. "Those were your very words. And now that you've dragged me out on this wild-goose chase—"

Paul burst out laughing. "You mean, tame-rooster

chase." Orson rolled his eyes and turned his back on Paul.

"Okay, listen up everybody!" Sergio's voice boomed through the bullhorn he was holding.

Where did everybody get all this stuff? Paul wondered. Pith helmets, capes, bullhorns, deerstalker caps? His schoolmates might be strange, but they were certainly resourceful.

The younger boys milled around Sergio excitedly. He unfolded a large square of paper and held it up. "This is a map of the Burnside campus. We are here." He pointed to a large red X on the map.

"We're going to divide the search area into sectors," he went on. From here to the stable is Sector One. From here to Pickles's house is Sector Two . . . "

Orson groaned quietly as Sergio described each of the ten sectors.

But Paul was impressed. It was the most talking Sergio had ever done, and the most confident he'd ever seemed. He might be miserable in a classroom, but he sure knew how to run a search party.

He divided the group into pairs and assigned each pair one of the ten sectors. Unfortunately, by the time everyone was paired off, the boys had forgotten where the sectors were.

Sergio, looking disappointed, ended up by simply pointing. "You go that way, you go this way, you go over there."

Since they had no walkie-talkies—another disappointment for Sergio—he would announce where he was every five minutes on the bullhorn. If anyone found Doodle, one of the team would stay with the rooster, and the other would run to alert Sergio. Wendell Warren, who was standing sadly off to one side, holding Doodle's cage, would follow Sergio and the scout to the area of the sighting.

"We'll muster back here at fifteen hundred," Sergio announced, "whether or not you've found anything."

"What's fifteen hundred?" Pinky asked.

"Three o'clock," said David.

Sergio sighed. "An hour from now."

"I don't have a watch," said Jonathan.

"This is the lamest re-con mission I've ever been on!" Sergio exploded.

"This is the only re-con mission you've ever been on," Orson snapped back. "Let's just get it over with already." He stalked off toward his sector, slogging through a mud puddle. Jonathan, his partner, cried, "Wait for me!" He hurried after Orson, stamping right through the same mud puddle.

Paul was teamed with Chris. "We've got the area around Bucky's house," Chris said. "That's past the stable. Practically in the woods."

"Bucky has his own house?" Paul asked.

"I wouldn't call it a house," Chris said. "It's more like a single-story slum."

They passed the corral behind the stable and Chris pointed. "Over there. Behind the willow tree."

Paul peered toward the leafless tree. It was huge,

and the willow wands, even without their leaves, were impossible to see through.

"Do you think we should be making rooster sounds?" Paul asked as they slogged over the squishy ground toward Bucky's house.

"You can if you want to," said Chris. "But I don't think you're going to fool the rooster."

Paul could hear some cockadoodledoo-ing in the distance. It sounded pretty stupid. If he were a bird, he wouldn't fall for it.

Chris led him past the willow. "There it is."

"Good grief." Paul stared. "Somebody *lives* there?"

Bucky's house was a wooden shack that leaned sideways, as if it had been built on a slantboard. It looked to Paul as if it might fall over and collapse in a heap of rotted wood if he sneezed on it.

There was one window. Right in the middle was a jagged hole, as if Bucky had hit it with a hammer.

"He doesn't have much luck with windows, does he?" Paul commented, thinking of the window in his room, which was still covered with cardboard.

The roof was made of linoleum. It had a multicolored spatter pattern, the kind you might find on a kitchen floor.

"I'll check inside," Chris said. "You look around out here."

Paul shook his head. "Not even a rooster would be stupid enough to go into that place."

"Well, there's that hole in the window," Chris said,

"so he could have flown in by mistake." He knocked on the door.

Paul jumped back, expecting Chris's tap to send the shack crashing to the ground.

"Bucky!" yelled Chris. "Are you home?"

There was no answer. He turned the doorknob.

"You're not going to break in, are you?" Paul asked.

"Are you kidding? This place is already broken." The door creaked as Chris pushed it in.

Paul shrugged. Chris had sneaked into Pickles's house. Why shouldn't he break into Bucky's? At least he was an equal-opportunity breaker and enterer.

Paul headed further into the woods, peering around for Wendell Warren's rooster. "Doodle," he called softly. "Oh, Doooodle." He felt really stupid, even though no one could hear him. So he switched to "Here bird. Here bird."

But there was no sign of Doodle. He bent over and searched the moist ground for signs of rooster tracks, but all he saw was a lot of dead leaves and rotting ferns.

Poor Wendell, he thought. They really ought to be searching Swenson's kitchen, not Bucky's place. After all, no one but Wendell Warren would want to keep a rooster for a pet, so the cook had the best motive for birdnapping. Wendell had already feared the worst before, when they'd had chicken nuggets for lunch. Maybe this time his fears were justified.

Hearing a distant bleating noise he straightened up. For a moment he wondered what the strange sound was. Then he realized it was Sergio, announcing his position on the bullhorn.

He had no idea where Sergio was. He couldn't understand a word he was bleating. It didn't make much difference, though. Doodle wasn't out here, and Chris hadn't come running out of the shack with a rooster under his arm. So they had nothing to report to Sergio.

But just then Chris did come running out of the shack, his face wild with excitement. "Tanner! You won't believe it!"

"Did you find him?" asked Paul.

"No, but look what I did find!" Chris waved something in the air. It looked like a bunch of pages from a small book.

"It's the photos!" he said. "From *Murder and Madness in Minnesota!*"

"Holy cow!" Paul snatched the pages from Chris. He only had time to glance at them, because Chris grabbed his arm. "Come on, hurry up," Chris said. "We've got to go back in there."

"Why?"

"We have to find Bucky's bankbook," Chris replied.

"Why do we have to find Bucky's bankbook?"

"Because Bucky is blackmailing Pickles, and the proof will be in the bankbook. I'll bet there's a regular pattern of deposits—hey, Tanner, don't you ever watch TV?"

"Holy cow." Paul couldn't think of anything else to say.

"And wait'll you see the inside of this dump," Chris said.

Numbly, he followed Chris into the shack. He forgot that he was afraid it would fall on him and kill him. He forgot Doodle and Sergio. He even forgot to worry that Bucky might catch them going through his belongings.

All he could think of was that the headmaster of his school was a Killer on the Loose.

Until he got inside the shack. Then, stunned, he did a three-sixty, staring at what Bucky had stored inside his hovel.

"I don't believe it," he breathed.

"I told you," Chris said smugly.

Bucky's furnishings included a full stereo setup, with a compact disc player, a video camera, a giant-screen TV, and a smaller TV with a built-in VCR. Propped against one wall was an inflatable raft, and next to it, three very fancy-looking fishing rods. Spread out along the opposite wall was a full set of power tools that looked as if they had never been used.

They'd certainly never been used to fix anything at Burnside, Paul thought.

Next to a small refrigerator were a microwave oven and two towering stacks of beer that reached almost to the ceiling.

Chris opened the refrigerator. It was crammed with beer bottles.

"No wonder he can't fix anything," Chris said.

Paul exhaled slowly. "How could he afford all this stuff?"

"There are three possibilities." Chris closed the refrigerator. "One: He stole it. In which case, he wouldn't leave his door unlocked so that we could walk in and see the loot. Two: Pickles pays an enormous salary to a man who can't fix a leaking faucet without destroying an entire bathroom. Or, three—"

"He's blackmailing Pickles," Paul finished. He looked around the shack again. Except for a battered table and chair and a narrow bed, there was no other furniture in the room. How could there be? Every inch of space was taken up with state-of-the-art consumer goods.

"How are we going to find a bankbook in here?" he asked. "If he's that careless about leaving the door open, he must have it pretty well hidden."

"Maybe he's careless about the bankbook, too," Chris said hopefully. "Considering how much beer he must drink . . ."

Now, finally convinced that Chris was right, Paul began to get a very unpleasant feeling in his stomach.

"Don't you think we ought to get out of here?" he said. "I mean, if Bucky is blackmailing Pickles, and he finds us—"

"Yeah, you're right," Chris said. "Even without a bankbook, all this stuff is proof that Bucky's getting a lot of money from somewhere."

Another blast of the bullhorn. Sergio was announcing his position again. Paul still couldn't understand what he was saying.

"And unless he hid it somewhere really corny," Paul went on nervously, "like under the mattress or something . . ."

He and Chris looked at each other.

"Nah," said Chris.

"Nah," Paul agreed.

They both dove for the bed. Paul stuck his hand under the mattress. His mouth dropped open in shock. He pulled out his hand. He stared, unbelieving, at the sheaf of hundred-dollar bills he was clutching.

He was still staring at them as the door flew open and Bucky staggered into the shack.

"Bucky!" shrieked Chris, jumping in front of Paul. "What are you doing here?"

Paul didn't know how to faint, but he figured he would learn in about ten seconds. The sheaf of bills felt as if it were burning his hand. He stuffed the money into his back pocket.

"I live here!" Bucky roared. "What in dangnation are *you* doing here?"

"Uh, looking for Doodle," Chris said quickly.

Bucky glowered at him. "What's a doodle?" he demanded. "And why are you looking for it in my house?"

"We're looking everywhere," Chris said. "We thought he might have flown in your window."

Bucky headed for the refrigerator. "Consarn kids," he growled. "Got some nerve breakin' into a man's house . . ." He reached into the refrigerator. While his back was turned, Chris whirled around and shoved Paul toward the bed.

Paul snatched the money out of his pocket, bent down, and stuffed it back under the mattress. He straightened up just as Bucky pulled a beer out of the refrigerator and slammed the door.

"Ought to call the cops," Bucky said. "Ought to have you arrested for trespassin'."

"Uh, you don't really want to do that, Bucky, do you?" Chris said. "We're sorry, and we'll never do it again as long as we live. Will we?" He turned to Paul.

"Never!" Paul said. "*Never.*"

Bucky stumbled over to the table. "Awwr, get outta here," he said. He fell into a chair. "Consarn kids ought to be horsewhipped."

Chris grabbed Paul's arm and dragged him to the door. Paul's legs weren't working very well, but the moment Chris pulled him outside, he started to run.

He didn't stop until he was inside his room, sprawled gasping across his bed.

"Now look." Chris held his hand over the lower part of the photo. It was two hours later. Paul was still shivering. "Just shave off the beard, and it's Pickles."

Orson peered at the photo. "It might be," he finally admitted. "It just might be."

"Hah!" Chris was triumphant. "So I'm not just imagining things."

"You're imagining things all the time, Bishop," Orson retorted. "But this time . . . I don't know."

They passed the photos back and forth. There were several pictures of Dwight Popper with captions underneath: "The murderer just before he escaped police custody." "Popper and his wife at a church breakfast." "Dwight Popper and his family vacationing at Lake Wickiup State Park camping grounds."

There were other pictures. The funeral, with Mrs. Popper's mother, Lana, looking angry, and "The grisly murder scene inside the modest ranch house."

Paul shuddered. Even Orson now believed Pickles was a murderer. If he'd wasted his own family, what might he do to someone who tried to expose him?

"We have to make a plan," Chris said. "We've got to nail this guy before he goes berserk again."

"I guess we do," Orson agreed. "I'm not going to have much fun being incorrigible if I have to worry about Pickles disciplining me with an axe."

Wendell Warren sat, glum and silent, in a corner of the room. Doodle had not been found. He hadn't been dinner, either. Dinner was franks and beans and the inevitable sauerkraut.

But that didn't make him feel any better. Tomorrow there might be chicken surprise for lunch.

Trying to get Wendell Warren's mind off his rooster, Paul turned to him. "You'll help us, won't you, Wendell? We're going to expose Mr. Pickles."

"Doodle was my best friend," Wendell said. He stared at the floor. "I was teaching him to shake hands."

How could you teach a rooster to shake hands? Paul wondered. He didn't have any hands to shake.

"I think I have an idea," Orson said slowly.

"To find Doodle?" asked Wendell.

"No, to blow Pickles's cover."

Wendell turned away. He gazed despondently at Orson's poster of Daffy Duck.

"Remember how in *Hamlet* they put on a play and act out Hamlet's father's murder?" Orson said.

"No," said Chris.

"You know," Orson insisted. " 'The play's the thing to catch the conscience of the king.' "

"No," Chris repeated.

"I saw part of *Hamlet* on TV once," said Paul. "I remember it."

"That's what we'll do," Orson said. "We'll re-enact *Murder and Madness in Minnesota*. In front of the whole school. In front of *Pickles*."

"Won't that be kind of dangerous?" Paul asked.

"What's he going to do, kill us all? And when he sees that we know who he is," Orson went on, "he'll crack, and give himself away."

"That's a great idea!" Chris said.

"I'll write the play," Orson said. "I'll direct it, too."

Paul frowned. "I'm not very good at acting," he said. "I don't think I could memorize lines."

"Don't worry," said Orson. "I'll also be the star."

Paul grinned. "For some reason," he said, "that doesn't surprise me a bit."

12

SHOCKING SECRET TO BE REVEALED AT FOUNDER'S DAY MASQUERADE!!

WATCH THIS SPACE FOR FURTHER DEVELOPMENTS!!

The next two weeks went by in a blur. Every moment that they were not in class, the boys worked on Orson's play.

Sergio's sewing machine hummed well into the night. He'd phoned in a rush order to the Wide World of Fabrics, and began cutting patterns the moment his material arrived.

Paul and Chris helped him with the cutting. Wendell Warren was supposed to be helping, too, but he was too depressed to be of much use. He carried Doodle's empty cage around with him wherever he went. He was acting so morbid that the boys didn't trust him with scissors.

Orson and Chris were printing the play on Chris's computer as Orson was writing it. Which meant that the actors were only getting their parts a page at a time. No one, except Orson, knew how the play would end, or how long their parts would be.

Paul suspected that even Orson wasn't sure. He was skimming *Murder and Madness* as he wrote the script. He never spoke up in classes anymore. He just scribbled, all the way through math, Latin, and English.

He didn't hold auditions for the parts, either. He simply assigned the roles and ordered the boys to study them.

Paul was stunned to find that Orson wanted him to play Pickles.

"I thought you were going to be the star," he protested.

"I was going to," Orson said, "but I'm going to have to direct this epic. And when I realized I'd be perfect for the part of J. Edgar Hoover, and I can't very well arrest *myself*—"

"Who's J. Edgar Hoover?"

"For heaven's sake, Tanner," Orson said. "He was the head of the F.B.I. for forty years. Sergio's making me this great double-breasted suit—"

"But I can't memorize," Paul said.

"That's okay," Orson assured him. "You can hold the script. We don't have enough time to make this perfect."

"But I don't think I can act," Paul went on. The thought of getting up in front of the whole school and acting out the murder of Pickles's family was terrifying.

"You'll be great." Orson clapped him on the shoulder. "You have star quality. I can sense that kind of thing."

"I have?" Paul was bewildered. "How can you tell?"

"You can read an entire sentence without mispronouncing any words," Orson replied. "Around here, that passes for star quality."

Jonathan and David were to play Pickles's children. They were very excited about being in the play until they found out that Orson wanted them to wear dresses.

"No way!" shrieked Jonathan. "I'm not going to be a girl!"

"Me neither!" agreed David.

Orson frowned. "All right. You can wear jeans. But you're girls, and your names are Daisy and Dinah."

David and Jonathan held a huddled consultation.

"Dirk and Dack," Jonathan announced when they came out of the huddle. "Not Daisy and Dinah."

"Daisy and Dinah," Orson insisted. "This is a true story. You *have* to be Daisy and Dinah."

They shook their heads stubbornly.

"Everyone in the play is going to be paid a hundred dollars," Orson said.

"A hundred dollars!" Jonathan and David put their heads together again, but this discussion took only seconds.

"Okay," they chorused. "We'll be Daisy and Dinah."

"For a hundred bucks I'll even wear a dress," Jonathan added.

"Why did you tell them that?" asked Paul, after the

boys left. "You're not going to give them a hundred dollars, are you?"

"Sure I will," said Orson. "After I sell the TV rights."

Nobody else but Chris, Sergio, and Wendell Warren knew that the play was about Pickles. Orson told everyone else that it was an original thriller, an Orson Autrey Production that would be presented during the annual Founder's Day masquerade.

It was Burnside's forty-ninth anniversary, and Sergio told Paul that the costume party was an annual celebration.

"Maybe we could ask the girls from St. Margaret's to come," Paul suggested when he heard about the masquerade.

"You'll have enough to do," Orson said, "without the merengue."

They started rehearsing only four days before Founder's Day. Orson had barely managed to finish the play the night before.

The first rehearsal was terrible. They used the stage in the auditorium, and the only person who really got into his part was Wendell Warren.

He was playing Amanda Popper, the killer's wife. Apparently he enjoyed screaming and flopping to the floor as Paul bonked him with a cardboard hatchet. It seemed to be the most fun he'd had since Doodle disappeared.

The second rehearsal was terrible. Paul hadn't been able to memorize his lines. Neither had anybody else. And it was awkward holding the script in one hand

and bludgeoning Wendell Warren with the hatchet at the same time.

"You're not violent enough," Orson criticized. "You're supposed to be insane with rage."

"If I hit him too hard, the hatchet bends," Paul said. "It's going to look ridiculous."

"Don't worry about petty details," Orson instructed. "Just be bloodcurdling. If you're bloodcurdling enough, no one's going to be looking at the hatchet. Especially after Wendell squirts the ketchup."

So Paul concentrated on being bloodcurdling. At first he felt self-conscious. He was a quiet, mild-mannered person, usually. How, he wondered, could he act like a homicidal maniac? Especially in front of an audience. Orson really should have picked someone else for the part.

But after a while, he began to think of all he had been through at Burnside. He thought of speed showering, checkers matches in a blizzard, Pickles's nasty, narrow face hovering over him while he tried to talk to his mother on the phone. He thought of sauerkraut casseroles and succotash soup, Pickles's brimming refrigerator, and mucking out Barbara Catalina's horse's stall.

He looked at Wendell Warren, and saw Pickles's face looming up at him.

"YAHHHH!" He swung the hatchet at Wendell's neck. Even after Wendell dropped, he kept hacking at the twitching body, his shrieks echoing horribly in the empty auditorium.

When he turned toward Jonathan and David, they screamed. They were supposed to scream. But this was the first time they screamed without giggling. They were still screaming as they ran to hide backstage.

Orson stood up and cheered. "Bravo! Star quality, Tanner. I *knew* it."

Paul flushed proudly. "Was I bloodcurdling enough?" he asked uncertainly. It felt strange to go so quickly from being himself to being a vicious killer and back again.

"My blood," Orson said with a dramatic shudder, "has never been more curdled."

Paul was so nervous and excited about the Founder's Day masquerade and Orson's play that he hardly had time to think about his parents' visit.

He still didn't know exactly when they'd arrive, but he was almost relieved on Founder's Day morning when they hadn't gotten there yet. Orson would never forgive him if they yanked him out of Burnside before he got a chance to perform in the play.

Mrs. Stern had been delighted to hear that Orson wanted to present his production during the party. Especially when he described it as an updated version of *Hamlet*. "Mr. Pickles was surprised that you're doing something so ambitious," she told Orson.

"He'll be even more surprised when he sees it," Orson promised.

That night Paul was so jittery he could hardly eat dinner. Which was just as well, because dinner was lamb stew. It smelled just as hideous as it had the first day he'd arrived at Burnside.

"Eat a few bites," urged Orson. "It'll really give you the urge to kill."

"It'll give me the urge to throw up," Paul said.

Sergio wasn't even at dinner. He was putting the finishing touches on the costumes. At one point during the meal, Chris disappeared for fifteen minutes. When he returned, he had a very mysterious smile on his lips.

A big, computer-printed banner stretched above the stage of the auditorium.

FOUNDER'S DAY—BURNSIDE ACADEMY—49 YEARS!!

The teachers were all lined up at the doors as the boys filed into the auditorium. They were in costumes, too. One was wearing an Elizabethan gown with a very tall neck and a white ruff. She had no head—at least, not on her shoulders. She held a wig model with flowing brown hair and a painted face tucked underneath her arm.

"Weird," Paul whispered to Orson.

"It's the beau of the ball," the headless woman said. The muffled voice came from somewhere inside her collar.

"Miss Twilley?" Paul asked.

The wig nodded.

"I didn't recognize you without your head," he said.

She giggled. "I'm Anne Boleyn. One of Henry the Eighth's wives. I was beheaded."

"Neat costume," Paul said.

"And I know who *you* are," she said slyly.

Paul was wearing a custom-made, Sergio original black suit with a white shirt. The string tie around his neck was a lace from Sergio's combat boots.

In his pocket he had a fake beard, which he would put on later for the play.

"I hope he won't be mad," Paul said.

"On no," said Miss Twilley. "Someone dresses up like him every year."

Mrs. Stern was Joan of Arc. Mr. Pigeon was wearing tights and a short jacket. He also had a wig. It was parted in the middle. The hair came down past his chin.

"Shakespeare," Orson said. Mr. Pigeon nodded, pleased that Orson had recognized him.

"Could have fooled me," Paul whispered. "I thought he was Joan of Arc, too."

Coach Waldrup wore a flowing white sheet that Paul guessed was supposed to be a toga. He had a wreath of gold leaves around his head.

"Hail, Caesar," Orson greeted him.

Coach raised one hand. "*Ave atque vale,*" he replied. It sounded like "ah-way ot-kway wah-lay."

"Pig Latin?" Paul asked.

"Real Latin," Orson said. "It means hail and farewell."

How appropriate, Paul thought.

"Who are you supposed to be?" Coach asked.

Orson was wearing a brown double-breasted suit and a brown felt fedora hat. He had a big gold badge pinned on his lapel.

"J. Edgar Hoover," he said.

"Very imaginative," said Miss Twilley's neck.

Paul and Orson moved away from the teachers as other boys pushed past them. Paul looked around at the array of costumes. There was a great variety of outfits. Some were very elaborate, and some just looked like leftovers from Halloween.

One boy was wearing David's Baltimore Orioles uniform. Pinky Lattimore wore a hospital gown and sweat socks. He had a metal band around his forehead, and he'd gelled his hair so it stood up straight all over his head.

He waved to Paul and Orson and trotted over.

"What are you supposed to be?" Paul asked.

"I'm a mental patient," Pinky said proudly. "Getting shock treatments."

"Couldn't hurt," Orson agreed.

Pinky crossed his eyes and let his tongue droop from his mouth. Then he turned and staggered off. Paul could see his underwear where the gown gaped in the back.

Sergio, Chris, and Wendell Warren came in together. Wendell Warren was wearing a flowered dress and a white apron. Chris wore an old-fashioned black dress with a ruffled collar and a black hat. His face was covered with a black chiffon veil. He was Wendell's mother in the play.

Neither of them seemed to mind dressing like girls. Wendell Warren was still rather depressed, but at least he wasn't carrying Doodle's cage with him.

"You look like you're going to a funeral," Coach Waldrup said to Chris.

"Could be," Chris said. "*Somebody's* funeral." Paul could only imagine his satisfied grin behind the veil.

Jonathan and David trailed after Sergio. They had reached a compromise about their costumes, but their faces were sulky.

They wore pajamas with feet. Jonathan's pajamas had little yellow ducks on them. David's had a picture of a teddy bear on the chest.

They stomped over to Orson and glared at him.

"Don't they look cute?" Orson beamed. "This is even better than dresses. They'll look really pathetic when they're murdered."

"We'll look·like dorks," Jonathan said.

"But pathetic dorks," Orson assured them.

Sergio was the biggest surprise of all. He was wearing a Burnside blazer and gray slacks. It was the first time Paul had ever seen him in the school uniform.

"How come you're not in costume?" Paul asked.

"For him, that *is* a costume," Chris said.

A large leather case hung from a strap around Sergio's neck. It looked somewhat like a camera case, but bigger.

"What's that?" Paul asked curiously.

"You'll see," Chris said, before Sergio could reply.

Mrs. Stern walked over to the boys. "When do you want to present your play?" she asked Orson.

"I guess in about half an hour," he answered.

"An hour," Chris corrected him.

"The sooner the better," Paul muttered. At the mention of the play his stomach lurched. He hadn't seen Mr. Pickles yet, but once Mr. Pickles saw his costume . . . He shuddered.

"Trust me," Chris said. "An hour. Eight-thirty."

"Okay." Orson nodded. "Eight-thirty, then." As Mrs. Stern walked back to the doors, he said, "Everybody be in the wings by eight twenty-five. Break a leg."

Paul headed for the refreshment table that had been set up in front of the stage. It was swarming with pirates, ghosts, hoboes, wild animals, and, he saw happily, three other boys in black suits and string ties.

The kids who hadn't been able to eat the lamb stew were scarfing down cookies and Kool-Aid. A boy in a gorilla suit smashed a handful of potato chips against his mask.

"Me want banana!" he growled. "Me want *banana!*" Paul edged away from him and tried to reach the Kool-Aid. His stomach was still feeling touchy, but he was thirsty.

Above him he heard a soft thunking noise, like someone tapping on a microphone. He looked up and saw that it *was* someone tapping on a microphone.

Mr. Pickles was standing on the stage, his wife on one side of him, Barbara Catalina on the other.

Barbara was dressed like a jockey.

Naturally.

For the first time Paul thought about the effect Orson's play was going to have. It wasn't just Pickles whose life would be changed forever. What would happen to Mrs. Pickles and Barbara? Even though Barbara no longer made his heart flutter, he *had* once cared about her.

Their happiness—if they *were* happy—would be destroyed when Pickles was exposed. Paul couldn't imagine that anyone would actually like living with Pickles, but he probably treated his family better than he treated his students. He certainly fed them better.

And what if, in spite of all the evidence, Chris was wrong? What if Bucky were a thief, not a blackmailer, and had simply stolen all those things they'd found in his shack?

What if the photographs had just fallen out of a copy of *Murder and Madness in Minnesota* that Bucky happened to be reading? Sometimes whole clumps of pages got loosened and fell out of paperback books if you read them too often.

Could you sue kids for libel? If Pickles was innocent, could he have Orson and Paul and the whole cast thrown in reform school because they defamed his character?

Or would he sue their parents? Would Paul's mother

and father have to pay him ten million dollars, and lose their new business and have to live in poverty for the rest of their lives?

He could manage only a few sips of Kool-Aid. He put the paper cup back on the table. He tried to blend in with the three other boys in black suits, and hoped Pickles wouldn't be able to pick him out of the crowd.

But Pickles would have no problem recognizing him once he was on stage.

He wished he were anywhere but here.

"Teachers, students, members of the Burnside family," the headmaster began. He held up his hands to signal for quiet. The boys didn't stop jostling around the refreshment table, but they jostled silently.

"I want to welcome you to the forty-ninth annual Burnside Academy Founder's Day celebration."

He waited for a cheer. Some of the teachers applauded politely, but not too enthusiastically.

"As I look out on all your faces tonight—even though I don't recognize all of them in those dandy costumes—I feel proud to be associated with such a fine institution of learning."

This time even the teachers didn't applaud. Some of the boys snickered.

"Here at Burnside we are constantly striving to bring out the best in our students," he went on.

Pinky Lattimore and the gorilla were trying to stamp on each other's feet.

"We try to develop boys who are not just academically excellent, but morally strong."

Paul thought his morals had grown weaker since he'd been at Burnside. He'd been involved in two house break-ins, went to sleep every night staring at the naked silhouette of Ursula Major, lied to Barbara about liking horses, and drenched himself with sexy after-shave to attract girls.

And academically—he didn't even want to think about how his brain must have deteriorated in Burnside's classrooms.

" . . . so let's begin the festivities," Pickles was saying, "by singing the Burnside alma mater."

He pulled a pitch pipe from his pocket and sounded a note.

"Hmmmm."

Paul hadn't known Burnside had an alma mater. He listened as the boys joined halfheartedly in the singing.

> *Burnside, Burnside we are loyal*
> *Always to maroon and gray.*
> *We will strive to live our lives*
> *Forever in the Burnside way.*

Heaven forbid, Paul thought.

After the alma mater, Mr. Pickles told the boys to find seats.

The teachers took to the stage.

Mr. Pigeon recited the soliloquy from *Hamlet*. " 'To be or not to be, dat is duh question. Wedder 'tis nobler . . . ' "

Nervous as he was, Paul had to cover his mouth to keep from laughing.

Coach Waldrup sang "Toot Toot Tootsie, Goodbye" in Latin. Mrs. Pickles accompanied him on the accordian. He had a pretty bad voice, but Mrs. Pickles played so loudly you couldn't hear very much of it.

Paul looked at the clock over the auditorium doors. Eight-fifteen. He didn't feel a bit like laughing anymore. Not even at a man in a toga singing "Toot Toot Tootsie" in Latin.

At eight-twenty, while a quartet of teachers dressed as sailors sang a medley of sea chanteys, Paul headed toward the side of the stage.

Orson, Chris, and Wendell Warren were already there. Jonathan and David were nowhere in sight. Maybe they didn't know how to tell time. Maybe they were hiding someplace. Maybe they just wouldn't show up.

Then Orson couldn't put on the play and Paul's parents wouldn't be sued for ten million dollars and he might get out of this horrible mess without ruining anyone's life.

But then he saw Sergio pulling the two boys toward the stage.

He tried to take a deep breath. There was a fluttering in his chest that made it hard to inhale normally. Between the chest flutter and the jumpy stomach, Paul didn't even know if he could make it back to the wings, let alone make it through the play.

But he had to. He was the star. And the show must go on.

13

"We have a special treat as part of our Founder's Day celebration," Mrs. Stern announced. "Orson Autrey has written a play based on Shakespeare's *Hamlet*—"

There was a chorus of groans from the boys, who hadn't expected anything educational to spoil the masquerade party.

She smiled. "But Orson has assured me," she said, raising her voice, "that it has plenty of blood and violence, so I know you won't be bored."

The groans turned to excited chatter. Mr. Pickles and his family sat down in the front row.

Does he have to sit *there?* Paul bit his lip. It would be bad enough to have Pickles staring at him during the play. But what if the re-enactment of his crime made him go berserk? What if he decided the show *mustn't* go on?

In two seconds he could reach the stage, grab Paul by the throat, and—

"Okay, everybody." Orson quickly handed out the scripts. "Here we go. Sergio, remember the curtain cues." Sergio nodded.

Orson strode to the center of the stage. "Ladies and gentlemen," he began. "The Orson Autrey Players present *Terror and Tragedy in Tallahassee.*"

Paul peeked out from the wings. Was it his imagination, or did Mr. Pickles's pale skin turn even paler? He gulped and squeezed his eyes shut.

"Written, produced, and directed by Orson Autrey. Starring Paul Tanner, Chris Bishop, and Wendell Warren Williams."

Paul opened his eyes. But he was afraid to look at the headmaster.

"The action begins in the quiet suburban home of a Florida high school teacher. But it doesn't stay quiet long. Act one: 'Tension in Tallahassee.'"

Orson bowed deeply. He walked offstage. Paul clutched the edge of the dusty curtain. He couldn't move.

"You're *on*," Orson gave him a little push.

"I—I—" He could see Pickles's face, ashen, eyes sunk deep in their sockets.

"Go!" Orson gave him a powerful shove, and he stumbled onstage. He stared out at the audience. His mouth worked, but nothing came out. Some of the boys started to giggle.

He clutched his script as if it were a life preserver. He could feel Pickles's eyes boring into him.

"*Go on!*" Orson hissed.

He took a deep breath. And, finally, got his first words out. "Bills, bills, bills!" He was supposed to sound angry, but his voice cracked. The words sounded like chicken squawks.

Paul tried to ignore the snickers. He waved the script around like a stack of letters. "Amanda! Come in here!"

Wendell Warren trudged onstage. He looked even heavier than usual in the flowered dress. The boys cheered and stamped their feet at the sight of him.

"What is it, dear?" he asked. He made no attempt to sound like a woman. He just talked in his regular voice.

"Amanda," Paul said, "I am merely an underpaid shop teacher. I cannot afford your extravagant tastes. We are already five thousand dollars in debt."

His voice grew stronger. As long as he didn't look at Pickles, he might be okay.

"Well, if you made a decent salary we wouldn't be in debt," Wendell Warren read from his script.

"My salary would be decent enough for a decent woman!" Paul bellowed.

"Whoo!" The audience reacted with cheers and whistles.

145

"What are you saying?" asked Wendell Warren. "That I am not a decent woman?"

"I warn you, Amanda, I cannot go on like this." Paul waved a threatening finger at Wendell. "Between your compulsive shopping and the children's wild ways, I am reaching a breaking point. There will have to be some drastic changes around here. *Or else.*"

Orson lowered the curtain. It was the end of act one.

Paul heard scattered applause as he ran offstage.

"Whew!" He fanned himself with his script.

"Great, just great!" Orson gloated. "You should see Pickles's face!"

"I'm afraid to look at him," said Paul.

Sergio was standing in the wings on the opposite side of the stage. Now Paul could see what he'd had in the carrying case around his neck. It was a video camera, just like Bucky's. But he wasn't filming the actors. He was pointing it at the audience.

Orson went back onstage to announce act two, "Trouble in Tallahassee." He ran back and raised the curtain. Jonathan and David dragged themselves onstage.

"Daddy's really mad about our report cards," Jonathan said.

"Yeah," said David. "That's why we have to go to bed so early." They were the only members of the cast who had managed to memorize their parts.

"I'm not sleepy," said Jonathan. He began to jump up and down, pretending he was on a bed.

"Me neither!" David started jumping also.

"Whee!" they yelled.

Paul flashed back to the night Bucky had come to fix the window. He remembered how Jonathan and Pinky had broken his bed, shrieking "Niagara Falls!" as they leaped around on it.

But this time Jonathan and David were yelling, "Trampoline! Trampoline!"

"That's your cue!" Orson said.

Paul shook his head to brush the memory away. He was careful not to look in Pickles's direction as he stalked onstage.

"Daisy! Dinah! Stop that this instant!"

The third graders shrieked with laughter when they heard the girls' names. Jonathan and David stopped jumping. They glowered at their classmates.

Paul pointed to his script. "These report cards are disgraceful. There'll be no more TV for you. And I'm taking away your Barbie dolls till you get your grades up."

The third graders hooted. "Barbie dolls?"

Jonathan's face was grim, but he carried on. "That's not fair!" he yelled, over the laughter.

"Yeah, you're mean!" David added.

"We hate you!" Jonathan stamped his foot.

"I am your father," Paul said sternly, "and you will obey me."

"No, we won't," Jonathan said. He and David began jumping again.

Paul tried to make his voice deep and frightening.

"Do you know what happens to little girls who don't obey their fathers?"

He must have sounded pretty scary, because no one laughed when he called Jonathan and David little girls.

"We don't care," said David. "Mommy says you might not be our daddy anymore."

Jonathan nodded. "Mommy said we might get a new daddy."

Paul gasped and clutched at his heart. "What?"

"So we don't have to listen to you," David finished.

Paul raised his fist in the air. "That wicked woman! That Jezebel! Oh, what an evil family!"

He dashed offstage as the curtain fell.

He could hear wild applause and cheers behind him. Jonathan and David followed him into the wings and confronted Orson.

"We want our hundred bucks," Jonathan said. "Now."

"We should get two hundred," David grumbled, "for having to look like dorks."

"You don't look like dorks," Orson said. "You're great. Listen to that applause."

"They laughed at us," David said.

"They love you," Orson argued. "And you don't get paid till the show's over."

Paul noticed that Chris was anxiously checking his watch.

"How does Pickles look?" Paul asked him.

"White as a sheet," he said. "Do you know what time it is?"

148

Paul looked at his own watch. "Eight forty-five. Why?"

"They should be here by now," Chris muttered.

"Who?" asked Paul.

"Everybody," he said mysteriously.

"Ready for the last act." Orson clapped his hands. "Wendell, don't forget your ketchup." Wendell Warren opened his fist to show him the little packet.

Orson stepped in front of the curtain. "Act three," he announced. *Terror and Tragedy in Tallahassee. 'The Final Chapter.'*"

Wendell, Paul, Jonathan, David, and Chris, who was playing Mrs. Popper's mother, took their places onstage. Orson stepped back into the wings and raised the curtain.

"I tell you, Lana," Paul said, "you have a wicked daughter and she is raising wicked children."

"The only wicked person around here is you, Dwight," Chris said. Paul couldn't help looking over at Pickles now. It was the first time they'd mentioned Dwight Popper by name.

Pickles was gripping the arms of his seat. He started to get up, then changed his mind. His mouth hung slightly open and his eyes were riveted to the actors.

Paul shivered.

"I told Amanda she never should have married you," Chris said. "She should have married Freddy Fleming when she had the chance."

"Freddy Fleming!" Paul shouted. "That four-flushing car washer!" The line had been a tongue twister in

149

rehearsal, but he got it out right. Some of the teachers laughed anyway.

"He's a millionaire today," Wendell Warren said. "He's got Minute Wash 'n' Wax franchises all over the country."

"Aha!" Paul cried. "So that's it! You're still seeing him!"

"If you must know," Wendell said, "Freddy has asked me to marry him again. And this time, I am going to accept."

"Never!" roared Paul. "You are *my* wife! You will never be anyone else's!"

No one was laughing now. The audience was absolutely still.

Paul raced offstage. He tossed his script aside, and Orson handed him the cardboard axe.

He ran back onstage waving the axe.

Chris screamed. He lifted the hem of his dress and ran. Wendell Warren screamed. Paul charged at him and brought the axe down on his head.

"Auugghh!" Wendell Warren grabbed at his head and squished the ketchup packet. The audience gasped as the fake blood spurted over his face and between his fingers.

Paul hit him again and he fell, gurgling, to the floor. Paul kept smacking him with the axe, like a madman. Wendell Warren twitched a few times, then lay still.

Orson had been right. Once they saw the ketchup, no one noticed that the axe was only cardboard.

"Now," Paul said, his voice a low growl, "to finish the job. Daisy! Dinah!"

"No! No! Stop this horrible travesty!"

Paul whirled around. Mr. Pickles was lunging toward the stage, his face red with fury.

At the same moment, a large crimson feathered creature swooped down from the rafters above the stage and landed on Wendell Warren's face.

"Doodle!" Wendell Warren sat up, completely forgetting he was supposed to be dead. "Doodle, you've come back to me!"

Some of the boys cheered, but most of the audience was staring, fascinated, at Mr. Pickles.

Just then the auditorium doors burst open and eight uniformed policemen charged down the aisles toward the stage. They were followed by five men in suits that looked a lot like Orson's costume.

Racing after them came a crew of people with video cameras, bigger than Sergio's, and a woman Paul recognized as one of the reporters from *Killers on the Loose*.

The auditorium erupted in chaos. Paul stood, dazed, not understanding anything that was going on around him. From a side door, he suddenly heard Bucky's hoarse voice. "Somebody stole my camera! Which one of you consarn kids pinched my camcorder?"

And behind everyone, looking stunned and confused, stood his parents.

Chris ran out from backstage. "There he is!" He

pointed at Mr. Pickles. "Dwight Popper! Killer on the Loose!"

The policemen and the men in suits swarmed toward the front row of seats. The TV people ran after them. Mrs. Pickles clutched at her throat. Barbara stared up at her stepfather, her eyes wide with horror.

"No, no! It wasn't me!" Pickles screamed. "I didn't do it!"

Orson jumped off the stage, flashing his badge. He clapped his fedora onto his head. "Hoover, F.B.I.," he shouted. "You're under arrest, Popper."

One of the men in suits pushed him away from Pickles. "Out of the way, kid. And Hoover's dead."

"At least I got to say my line." Orson smiled proudly.

Two uniformed policemen grabbed the headmaster's arms. They handcuffed his wrists.

"This is all a horrible mistake!" Pickles screamed. "It wasn't me! It was my twin brother! Him. *Him!*"

And he raised his cuffed hands and pointed at Bucky.

14

EVIL HEADMASTER'S SECRET IDENTITY REVEALED!!

PICKLES CRACKS UNDER QUESTIONING, ADMITS HARBORING FUGITIVE TWIN!!!

"Evil twin brother," Orson said disgustedly. "That is *so* trite."

"Trite but true," said Chris. He, Paul, and Orson sat in the common room. It was crowded with boys glued to the television set. They'd been watching the news for two days. Every time they saw their headmaster get handcuffed, they cheered. Every time they saw Bucky taken into custody, they yelled, "Yay, Bucky!"

When the news wasn't on, they watched Sergio's videotape. He had captured all of Pickles's reactions to Orson's play. Every time they saw his gaunt face they booed.

"But you were wrong, Bishop," Orson pointed out. Pickles wasn't Popper."

"Pickles *was* Popper," Chris insisted. "He just wasn't *Dwight* Popper."

"Oh, a minor point," Orson said sarcastically. "You accuse the wrong man of being a homicidal maniac. Oops."

"And we didn't even suspect Bucky," Paul said.

Chris shrugged. "He didn't look like his pictures. He doesn't even look that much like Pickles."

"Exactly my point," said Orson.

"And Pickles *is* a criminal," Chris reminded him. "He harbored a fugitive from justice. He'll probably be rooming with Bucky in the slammer."

"And Bucky wasn't even blackmailing Pickles," Orson said. "He stole credit cards. So you got that wrong, too."

"All right, all right," said Chris. "So he was a thief instead of a blackmailer. But we *still* captured a Killer on the Loose."

"Can you believe we got out of his house alive?" Paul felt a shiver at the back of his neck.

"If he'd been sober," Chris said, "we'd have been dead meat for sure."

"I wonder how we'll look on the show," Paul said. He and Chris had both been interviewed by "Killers on the Loose" after the arrests.

"Probably stupid for fingering the wrong guy," Orson said grumpily.

"Oh, you're just jealous because they only talked to you for two minutes," Paul teased him.

"Well, it was my idea that exposed them," Orson complained. "If it weren't for my play—"

"But *I* convinced them that Popper was here," Chris said. "*I* dug up all the evidence, *I* found enough proof to make them believe me, *I* made all the phone calls to the F.B.I. and the police, and—"

"And nobody even heard my line." Orson sighed.

"What'll happen to Mrs. Pickles and Barbara?" asked Paul.

"They didn't know anything about it," Chris said. "Nothing will happen to them."

"But what will they do?" Paul persisted.

"I don't know." Chris shook his head. "Maybe Mrs. Pickles will marry Freddy Fleming and Barbara can buy a whole stableful of horses."

"What'll happen to us is what I'm worried about," said Wendell Warren. He sat cross-legged, feeding Doodle sunflower seeds. "This is the only school I ever liked."

Pinky Lattimore snorted. "You're weird, Wendell, you know that?"

"Yeah, but everybody here is weird," Wendell Warren said calmly, "so I fit right in."

Paul grinned. But he didn't know what would happen, either, and he knew how Wendell Warren felt. His mother and father, along with a group of other parents, were meeting with Mrs. Stern in Mr. Pickles's former office.

Chris's parents were there, and Mr. and Mrs.

Williams, and Pinky's mother. Orson's parents were in Japan. Orson claimed that he didn't care what happened one way or the other, and it didn't bother him that his parents hadn't come.

But Paul didn't believe him.

Paul's mother and father had already told him that he could go to Switzerland with them if he wanted to. They were as shocked by the conditions at Burnside as they were to see the school's headmaster arrested.

So he knew that whether they closed the school or found a way to keep it open, he'd be okay. But he wasn't so sure about Orson.

"Look," said Pinky, "here they come."

A crowd of parents, led by Mrs. Stern, headed down the hall. They filled the common room. Right behind Mrs. Stern Paul spotted a familiar face.

"Uncle Jack!" He jumped up and ran to his uncle. He threw his arms around him.

"Hey, Paulie, how're you doing?" Uncle Jack planted a big kiss on his forehead.

Embarrassed, Paul dropped his arms to his sides.

"Boys, we have an announcement to make," Mrs. Stern began. "Mr. Jack Tanner, the uncle of one of our students, and a graduate of Burnside himself, has decided to make a *very* generous contribution to the school's endowment fund."

Some of the boys exchanged puzzled looks. Uncle Jack smiled and nodded.

"He is investing enough money in Burnside," she

went on, "so that we can keep the school open at least for the next year."

Half the boys in the room booed.

"But there will be some changes made," she said.

All the boys in the room cheered.

"We will be hiring some new teachers—"

Mixed cheers and boos. Paul was sure Miss Twilley would be replaced by a real math teacher. He realized he would miss her.

"—and revamping our sports program."

No more checkers in the snow. He wouldn't miss Coach Waldrup.

"I will serve as acting head. We're going to make all necessary repairs so that our school will be more pleasant and—um—livable."

Uncle Jack saving Burnside? Paul could hardly believe it. Maybe he felt responsible for Paul's being in such a terrible place. Maybe he felt guilty for recommending the school to the Tanners. Or maybe, as he'd said, he really had loved Burnside, and wanted other kids to love it, too.

Paul could hardly take it in. All around him the boys were buzzing with the news. Very soon he would have to decide whether he would stay at Burnside or go to Europe with his parents.

He was startled to realize that he wasn't sure he wanted to leave.

"What about the swill?" Orson's voice cut through the noise.

"Excuse me?" Mrs. Stern frowned.

"The food!" Orson, Chris, and Paul shouted it together, like the Three Musketeers.

Mrs. Stern smiled. "We will be getting a new dietitian and a new cook."

"YAY!" The boys leaped to their feet and rushed Mrs. Stern. They mobbed her like fans at a rock concert.

"STERN! STERN! STERN!" They began to chant.

Paul and Orson grinned at each other. Chris looked proud enough to burst.

"This is all because of me, you know," he reminded them. "And my—ahem—wild imagination."

"I think Paul's uncle deserves a little credit," Orson said.

"Yeah. It ought to be pretty cushy for you here with your uncle practically owning the school," Pinky Lattimore said. "I'll bet you could get away with murder."

"Not with Bishop around," Paul said. Chris patted himself on the back smugly.

"So what are you going to do?" Orson tried to sound casual, as if he didn't really care whether his roommate stayed or not.

Paul went over it in his mind again. His parents would only be in Europe for another month. Orson's new Spandex wings were almost completed, and spring was coming—good flying weather. And maybe another dance. St. Patrick's day was only twelve days away.

Pickles was gone, and Swenson was gone, and Uncle

Jack might hang around awhile to see how his money was being used.

He looked over at his parents, who were trying to work their way around the cluster of boys to reach him. Uncle Jack was bending down to talk to Jonathan and David, who were tugging at his sleeves.

Probably asking him for their hundred dollars, Paul thought.

What *do* I want to do? he wondered.

Even with a new head, new teachers, and edible food, Burnside would still be home to an extremely strange bunch of students.

But if he went to Europe, he would miss them. Odd as they were, they'd become his friends. He knew that if he left, he'd spend an awful lot of time wondering what they were doing. He'd want to know what changes Mrs. Stern was making, and how Chris was lying about them in the *Banner*.

His parents finally reached him. His mother grabbed him and gave him a hug. His father said, "This has been quite a couple of days, hasn't it?"

"For me it's been quite a couple of months," Paul reminded him.

"Well, it's over now," his mother said. "We can leave as soon as you're packed."

"I think I'm not leaving," he said.

"You're not?" His father looked stunned.

Chris and Wendell Warren cheered. Sergio thumped him on the back. "You're crazy, Tanner," Orson said.

"You've turned as warped as the rest of us. This place has destroyed your mind."

But he was grinning from ear to ear.

"Yeah," Paul agreed.

His parents looked at each other and shook their heads.

"I'm going to sort of miss Pickles, though," he said. "Without him to hate, the school just isn't going to be the same."

Uncle Jack climbed up on the piano bench. "And to celebrate our new beginning," he exclaimed, "let's all join in a rousing chorus of the Burnside alma mater!"

There was a deafening roar of boos from the boys. They charged at the piano bench like a herd of stampeding cattle.

"Or maybe it will," Paul said, and laughed so hard he had to lean on Orson to keep from falling down.